For Luca and Freddie

WONDERLANDS

CLARE COULSON

Photography by Éva Németh

Quadrille

CONTENTS

FOREWORD

One day in the 1990s, the garden designer Penelope Hobhouse answered the phone. 'Is that John Brookes?' asked a caller from America, looking for a British designer for his garden. 'No? Oh, yes you're the other designer in Britain. I've got both your names on this piece of paper.' There were, to be fair, more than two garden designers in Britain at that time. And the client was more than happy with the garden Hobhouse would go on to design for him – but the story serves to underline how the profession of garden design has expanded in the thirty years since.

There has never been so much talent working in the design of gardens; at no point since the Edwardian age is so much private money being spent on designed gardens. Clare Coulson chose a new route into this story: she chose to interview garden designers in their own gardens, beginning with Arne Maynard amused and amusing at the challenge of placing topiary – a masterful signature – against his house, Allt y Bela, as tall as a 'skyrocket'. (And in the process Éva Németh, her photographer collaborator, reveals an extra talent as a portraitist).

If there is one theme that connects designers acting as their own client it is a different relationship to time. You are not pushed into solutions, continues Maynard; for a while the forty yew trees he marshalled for his ochre skyrocket looked like a Christmas tree farm – but no matter. Coulson sees these gardens as places of 'slow evaluation'. But they are also uninhibited spaces to be impulsive: Sue Stuart-Smith remembers waking to the sound of chainsaws early one Saturday morning. Her husband Tom had decided to rip out a rose garden established at their Hertfordshire garden, and put in a design of planting and Corten steel. It is with a similar freedom that in 2011 he added a half-acre prairie with a mix created by James Hitchmough, which was a chance to indulge experiments in pure colour, and to enjoy surprise. While in a former quarry in the Peak District, Nigel Dunnett can garden uncompromised to his credo of 'if it doesn't survive, don't keep it'; the necessary converse of his respect for the independent identities of species. (And he took from a book by Humphry Repton, the device of planting three young trees in one hole: would you tell that to a client?).

Gardens have a unique sense of time, where past, present and future merge; in no other activity, I think, is there such depth of time in a pick of an apple, or the glint of an unburied bulb. In Wales, Sarah Price – eyes glancing away from her interviewer, always noticing something new in her own garden – has returned to her grandparents' home, but is also in unspoken conversations with her late father, with whom she loved to garden as a child. Above Bath, Dan Pearson's garden is a drawing together of travels, and mentors, in a site chosen, in part, because it is enclosed by hills on which nothing happens so never distracts from the deep sunk spell.

This relationship between the chance to experiment and the continuity of a personal style is seen at its most exquisite at Gresgarth Hall in Lancashire; here, Arabella Lennox-Boyd continues to plant new enthusiasms in trees and shrubs – inspired by adventures with the International Dendrology Society – but as if re-working, in detail, the same canvas. And so a modern masterpiece stays young.

And there is something else we are privileged to glimpse in this book. Harry Rich says 'we are quite quiet people and we like our personal space'. These are places of domestic happiness: the happy islands which explorers seek.

Christopher Woodward
Director, Garden Museum

INTRODUCTION

The ripples of influence from the world's leading landscape architects and garden designers stretch out exponentially, well beyond their hugely varied public spaces and private commissions. Their work shapes the approach to green spaces across the globe, but on a micro level they also influence how we design our own gardens and what we plant in them; a stand-out show garden, for example, can dictate planting palettes, design details or choice cultivars for years to come. But more profoundly, their work can help to popularise ideas around best horticultural practice, biodiversity, sustainability and planting for a better world.

Designers' own gardens can be distinctly different to those that they are commissioned to create for clients. They may be made without a masterplan, they are often a place where a slow evolution can happen without time constraints. It's in their own gardens where designers can closely observe plants or combinations, and ideas can be crystallised; their gardens are test beds, sometimes quite literally, but also a personal space that needs to function on a domestic scale too.

It's impossible to generalise the work of the landscape architects and garden designers in this book – or their personal domains; each one is as distinct as their wildly contrasting work – but there are threads that can be drawn between them.

Their gardens illustrate the way in which landscape design has evolved, especially over the past two decades when naturalistic planting and a more holistic approach towards wildlife and biodiversity have taken hold; it's rare to encounter a designer now where gardening sustainably and organically for nature is not a top priority. Responding to a changing climate is also a key concern, especially for designers who are working on a global scale, developing a resilient plant palette and planting practices that are future-facing; in several of the gardens in this book, designers such as Sarah Price experiment with planting into recycled sand or rubble, or use repurposed or experimental materials that leave a low carbon imprint.

Although these are private gardens, there is a sense in many of them of a greater good, whether that's through social enterprise, such as Tom Stuart-Smith's Serge Hill Project for Gardening, Creativity and Health where the garden becomes a community resource, or through a deep sense of land restoration where designers view themselves as stewards, restoring the earth and biodiversity. Many gardens in this book have been carved out from the most inauspicious plots, including concreted farmyards, or areas where wildlife has been obliterated after years of hard grazing.

For some designers such as Nigel Dunnett, whose fearless approach to his Peak District garden echoes his trail-blazing work in the public realm, the garden becomes a continual experiment with bioswales, mini meadows and areas that sit on the edge of wildness that defy our idea of what a garden is, or can be.

But these are, of course, also their private gardens, a refuge as well as a point of reference. Each one channels a specific sense of place, and each one has been created with determination, resourcefulness and ingenuity.

TOM STUART-SMITH

HERTFORDSHIRE

When Tom Stuart-Smith planted the gardens at his Hertfordshire barn in the early 1990s, his choices tended to lean towards giants – cardoons and towering wild fennel, vernonias and veronicastrums, species hollyhocks and *Macleaya cordata*, the spectacular plume poppy with its beautiful fig-shaped leaves. At 6 ft 5 in tall, Tom was not destined to be a fan of diminutive forms: 'I have always loved plants that look me straight in the face, that give me the feeling of being amongst it all', he explains in *The Barn Garden,* the 2011 book, co-authored with his wife Sue, that charts their garden's early development.

Fast forward 14 years and the borders that stretch out from the house are certainly immersive, a textural mass of soft and hazy forms that have grown shaggier over time, surrounded by cloud-pruned yew and, further away from the barn, more crisply angular hornbeam hedges that also enclose two serene lawns. When he first made the garden, Tom was in the grip of an Arts & Crafts obsession, but would be increasingly drawn to the naturalistic planting movement that was happening in Europe, spear-headed by designers and plantspeople including Piet and Anja Oudolf in Holland and Cassian Schmidt, who was then the director of Hermannshof, the show and trial gardens in Weinheim, Germany.

Those twin influences have informed many of his best-known projects, such as Trentham Gardens in Staffordshire, where a formal Victorian setting is contrasted with strong vertical forms and contemporary planting, or Broughton Grange in Oxfordshire where statuesque clipped beech topiary is set amongst soft billowing grasses and perennials that reach a ghostly peak in midwinter. 'I think I've always been a sort of sponge of influence', says Tom. 'I have learned a lot from other people, and seeing the results of gardens that I've made. But my garden has to be the foundation of my knowledge; it's definitely the thing that gave me confidence, it's the one that I've learned most from.'

The story of the garden begins almost a century ago in 1927 when his grandfather, Tom Motion, bought the Serge Hill estate. Part of that land would later become the designer's home and garden, and then his design studio, all created out of what was once an 'agri wasteland' as Tom describes it.

As a postgraduate landscape design student (he had originally studied zoology at the University of Cambridge), one of his theoretical plans was for a courtyard garden set in a collection of old pig sties, a milking shed and a decrepit 17th-century barn on the estate. When he married Sue in 1986, his parents offered the couple the barn as a home. His parents then proceeded to rebuild it themselves, cutting structural timbers, as well sycamore and oak for the floors, from the surrounding woodland.

Before creating the formal borders, the couple had made a rose garden in the inner courtyard, but in 2007 Tom completely redesigned this area using the long Corten steel wall and water tanks from his arresting 2006 gold medal-winning garden at the RHS Chelsea Flower Show. Around the reflective tanks the planting includes *Astrantia*, *Salvia* and sedums with metallic *Eryngium*, acid *Euphorbia* and textural grasses providing contrast. Above it all *Genista aetnensis* – the Mount Etna broom – produces great weeping sprays of intense yellow flowers in high summer.

'GARDEN DESIGN IS A LITTLE WORLD BUT IT'S ONE WHERE YOU CAN FEEL, AT LEAST ON A DAY-TO-DAY BASIS, HOPEFUL ABOUT WHAT YOU'RE DOING.'

In 2011, in addition to the six acres of wildflower meadows that sweep around the whole garden, he added a horseshoe-shaped half-acre prairie, sown with a seed mix devised with James Hitchmough, who collaborated on the planting for the 2012 London Olympic site. Like the rest of the area, which sits on glacial drift, part of the land is free-draining whilst elsewhere is more moisture retentive – the variable soil makes it very interesting to garden, says Tom. He designed the garden so that the predominant colours of yellow, purple and blue can be admired in all their backlit beauty when walking west through the garden at sunset: 'I don't generally garden for colour, but that was an instance where I did.'

Through each area of the garden it's possible to trace the development of Tom's design work. He'd already been gardening at Serge Hill for more than a decade when he formed his own studio in 1998, the same year that he made his debut at Chelsea with a baroque garden for Chanel – he has since won nine gold medals (the most recent a soothing woodland garden for the National Garden Scheme in 2024), and three 'best in shows'. He was awarded an OBE in 2023.

It's almost impossible to define the style of a designer whose work is truly international and responds to such a diversity of sites, often on an epic scale. He can take the simplistic – a reduced palette of a handful of plants in one of two gardens at Le Jardin Secret, Marrakesh for example – and transform it into something almost cinematic. There, an Islamic garden with citrus, pomegranate and olive trees is underplanted with a repeating palette of just three plants – *Stipa tenuissima*, *Lavandula dentata* and *Tulbaghia violacea*. It's a ravishing, hypnotic space.

His clients have included Queen Elizabeth II (he designed the Queen's Jubilee Garden at Windsor Castle), the Duke of Devonshire (a range of projects on the Chatsworth estate include a reimagining of a three-acre rock garden originally conceived by Joseph Paxton) and public projects at RHS Bridgewater, Hepworth Wakefield and a Jurassic garden of tree ferns for the Royal Academy in London. He is currently working on gardens for Tate Britain in London and, in the centre of Edinburgh, a garden for the National Centre of Music, around a neoclassical building that sits in a spectacular position on Calton Hill, above Holyrood and the bottom of the Royal Mile.

'I do feel more interested in doing those public spaces', explains Tom, who as a young designer thought he would specialise in gardens for social housing. 'But I wouldn't want to do all public because they take a long time.' Instead, his studio – which now has a team of 21 – works across private gardens and estates and commercial developments, as well as in the public realm. 'It's a huge responsibility, but it's also a huge gift to be in that position', he says of his ever-growing studio. 'And to be able to work with such talented, delightful and brilliant people.'

Over time his gardens have leaned more heavily towards the ecological – in 2022 the final planting was added to his 'rewilded' garden on the Knepp estate in Sussex, which experiments with resilient planting and recycled materials. But nowhere is this focus more apparent than in the latest addition to his own plot. In 2024 he added the site's most transformative addition to date – the Serge Hill Project for Gardening, Creativity and Health – a collaborative project with Sue, a psychiatrist and psychotherapist, and author of the 2020 best-selling book *The Well Gardened Mind*.

The one-acre plant library serves as an educational resource for school children, students, and the local community, to observe plants and their habits more closely. Currently there are around 1,600 plants, including herbaceous perennials, shrubs and bulbs, that are each allocated their own square metre, the vast proportion are planted into 20 cm (8 inches) of sand, with a shadier, damper area for plants that prefer those conditions. And there are now plans to expand the library further into a neighbouring paddock owned by Tom's sister, Kate.

Alongside the library, a local charity, the Sunnyside Rural Trust, trains people with learning disabilities to propagate plants, which can then be sold, in their purpose-built nursery. The central Apple House, designed by Tom's architect son, Ben, hosts workshops, lectures and events. It's a resource for the local community too with veg beds (including one that provides produce for the nearby design studio).

It all speaks to the transformative power of plants, and the potential in green spaces for the greater good. 'Garden design is a little world but it's one where you can feel, at least on a day-to-day basis, hopeful about what you're doing', adds Tom. 'And with a bit of luck, you're working somewhere where at the end of a working day, you feel you've gone a little way to making it a slightly better place in terms of gross domestic happiness.'

MIRANDA BROOKS

GLOUCESTERSHIRE

It's hard to know where to look as I am whisked up to the first-floor dressing room of Miranda Brooks' exquisitely decorated 17th-century farmhouse on the edge of the Slad Valley in Gloucestershire. Inside there are mesmerising details in all directions, but outside the land is calling.

To the east, a velvety lawn sweeps out below us, bordered by long meadow grass, enclosed by hedges of cloud-pruned yew and dissected with an avenue of box-pleached limes. As the lawn slopes away, yew obelisks add another punctuation point; a gateway leading the eye out into the distance. All around are adolescent trees (Miranda has planted thousands) that one day will spread out and ground this young landscape.

On the opposite side of the house, to the west, a courtyard, boundaried by mellow stone barns, is dotted with clipped yew topiary, roses, a quartet of pollarded mulberries and two low ovals of osmanthus. Along a gravelled path there are silvery Mediterranean plants and figs in a nod to Miranda's French architect husband, Bastien Halard.

Through a scallop-topped gate made, like so many things here, by Bastien ('He can build anything,' she says), there's an immaculate kitchen garden, arranged with cut-flower beds edged with woven hazel and frothing over with dahlias in coral, scarlet and rich dark reds, anemones and chocolate cosmos, with clipped beech topiaries standing sentinel in each corner. And on the opposite side, beds of deep green kale, cabbages, beans, carrots and herbs. Beyond it all there are tantalising views of the distant valley.

Although relatively new, this is a garden full of transporting views. But when they arrived here from Brooklyn with their two daughters in the winter of 2019, there was nothing of note in the garden. The land, hard grazed for decades as a dairy farm, was a blank canvas, and so too was the house, which had no architectural details or 'good rooms'. Bastien masterminded its renovation, with tactile surfaces and beautifully conceived and crafted details at every turn. 'After hundreds of years of being a very hard-working farmhouse, the house began to feel sort of pretty,' says Miranda. 'There's a language here that we're both trying to find all the time.' That consideration of materials, textures and how everything feels extends outside, too, so that each bench, weathered gate or stone step is carefully considered within the context of this landscape.

Their search for the house was exhaustive – and exhausting. For years holidays were spent scouring England for a suitable project before a friend, the artist Dan Chadwick, sent a blurry photo of the farmhouse that could soon be up for sale. On a walk with the writer Plum Sykes, she managed to take a sneak peek. 'There was masses of barbed wire, and all the tractors were parked on the side, and I saw into the courtyard, which was just concrete and bales of straw and machinery. But it was magic.' Back home in New York, she wrote to the owners but never heard anything back.

Two years later – and on the verge of giving up – she was visiting Sykes, who asked what had happened with the farm, and then persuaded her that they should go to the house right away. The owners remembered Miranda's letter but it hadn't been the right time to sell. Now things had changed. The following day they went back and shook on a deal in the field.

'AFTER HUNDREDS OF YEARS OF BEING A VERY HARDWORKING FARMHOUSE, THE HOUSE BEGAN TO FEEL SORT OF PRETTY. THERE'S A LANGUAGE HERE THAT WE'RE BOTH TRYING TO FIND ALL THE TIME.'

The tractors remain in the farmyard (collecting them is an obsession for Bastien) along with a collection of animals, including five horses, a flock of bantam hens, Indian Runner ducks, two fluffy cats, and three dogs, including the impossibly beautiful slate-grey whippet, Cuckoo.

Miranda, who is also a contributing editor at *American Vogue*, is something of an enigma. She is jaw-droppingly elegant (she is rarely out of her signature corduroy jodpurs that are as practical for riding as they are for gardening) and has a cool English reserve. She grew up on a small farm in Hertfordshire, where her American mother who, determined that she'd never have to visit a shop, ensured they were self-sufficient. 'I don't know how she did it, but it was always our own bread, our own butter, and we ate our own meat and and we were organic.' Gardening was sometimes administered as a punishment – but plants were also a refuge. By the time she was studying art history at the Courtauld Institute of Art in London, she would visit nurseries to decompress: 'I never connected that until so much later. It actually just made me feel good being around plants.'

On holiday one summer in the south of France she met David Chipperfield, who dispensed with any notion she had of training as an architect (like her father, John Sergeant) and instead proposed that she design landscapes. As part of her postgraduate degree in landscape architecture at Birmingham Univerity she apprenticed with Arabella Lennox-Boyd.

In the early 1990s as a newly trained designer, she moved to New York with her first husband, Christopher Brooks, and set up her own studio. There, she found making gardens was a very different ballgame, but she got her first break creating a garden for Anna Wintour in the West Village, which was followed by the scheme for Wintour's expansive country estate on Long Island.

Miranda's gardens are distinctive yet completely timeless. With their focus on evergreen structure, meadows and mown paths, tumbling roses and pretty plant palettes, her designs have a deep sense of the pastoral and an intense connectivity to nature. It's a style that she thinks emerged in some part due to her homesickness living as an expat in New York. 'I actually always wanted to be back,' she says. 'So I was trying to create something that felt softer and romantic and looser than you would typically see in America.'

Being based in New York came with its own challenges of a more limited plant palette and demanding climate, but it also put her at a distance from her design peers so that in many ways she was liberated to create her own aesthetic. Despite relocating to England, her business is still based in New York and her work life is spent on Zoom calls to her studio and clients, and on trips back to oversee projects.

And there are still many more plans for her own 36 acres, but this is also a shared endeavour for the couple; both of them are hands-on and practical, sculpting this land into a future idyll. For Bastien, who grew up in a botanical garden outside Paris and spent holidays in his grandparents' home, Châteaurenaud, in the middle of France, planting trees and working the land on tractors is a passion. He comes from a long, storied line of designers and decorators. 'But none of this did I really know,' reveals Miranda, 'when I met a 24-year-old Frenchman in New York.' In 2023 the couple launched their own collection of outdoor fabrics, Catswood.

As you'd expect in a household of designers, there are creative differences too. They've fought over the immaculate osmanthus ovals that bring graphic structure to the inner courtyard ('he thinks the courtyard should be empty'), and the proximity of a beguiling walled garden of single yellow roses, clematis, scabious, geraniums, *Selinum wallichianum*, *Alchemilla mollis* and *Valeriana officinalis* to the front of the house – named the 'granny garden' for its pastel palette. The colour-themed gardens, including a pretty red terrace close to the kitchen, are inspired by the chakras, and all of the land here is managed biodynamically.

To the south of the house, Miranda has added a calm and soothing garden in memory of her friend Stella Tennant, with multistem trees, clipped beech topiary and a curving landform surrounding a circular pool, designed to reflect the night sky. Soon after moving in, the couple installed a small lake high above the house, and they are currently grappling with the flow of water through the land – wherever they dig they seem to hit a natural spring. 'I've got this very misguided idea that we're in the hardest phase, because everything's young,' adds Miranda. 'And that once the wildflowers are more established, and once the trees aren't needing to be watered so much, it's going to become easier.' Like all of her projects, she is guided here by the spirit of the place and how the land speaks to her. 'Because I only want it to be right for the place, I'm not going in with an ego.'

DAN PEARSON

SOMERSET

Sitting in the open-sided barn adjoining Dan Pearson's stone farmhouse just a few miles outside Bath, it's hard to concentrate on the conversation at hand; there is drama unfolding across the valley, as giant marshmallow clouds throw enormous shadows onto the hills, while shafts of celestial sunrays break out across the endless skies to the west. The epic views, a tapestry of velvety greens typical of a sodden English midsummer, change minute by minute. Here, says Dan, 'The landscape is king.'

Two acres of cultivated areas stretch out from either side of the house, with expansive ornamental borders sloping down to the east, segueing gently into the hills beyond. On the opposite side of the house, the kitchen garden – one of the few flat spaces here, created using earth borrowed from land above – leads to the original barns, which are made from a rough patchwork of rusted corrugated panels. Beyond them is the latest addition at Hillside – a sand garden of Mediterranean plants that was added in 2023.

But in front of the house the land fades away into meadows, dissected with restored hedgerows and meeting a stream and woodland that marks the plot's boundary below. 'I didn't want us to look out from the house onto anything that felt cultivated,' explains the landscape architect, who moved here with his partner Huw Morgan in 2010. 'When we are in this little barn, we want to look out onto something that doesn't feel like it's beckoning us to do something.'

They'd been searching for a property for six years when, in 2010, an old friend – who now shares their boundary – tipped them off about the farm that was about to come on the market with the words, 'It's nothing special, but it's a nice piece of land.' In February, they walked down from their friend's house, which is on the darker north side of the valley, through the wood, over the stream, and finally up into winter sunshine. 'The views just sort of revealed themselves and opened up,' Dan recalls. 'We took about half an hour to decide that we were going to do it. We didn't even say, "shall we do it?" We just said, "how can we do it?"'

They moved in that autumn and spent six years living in the existing unmodernised two-up, two-down farmhouse, while observing the surrounding 20 acres that had been grazed hard by the farmer and his beef cattle for decades. They began repairing hedges, oversowing meadows with a local wildflower seedmix, St Catherine's, and planting many trees, including a blossom wood that sits above the house, and an orchard lower down on the plot, both of which now have a real presence on the land. There was little birdsong or signs of life when they arrived, but it swiftly returned as the hedges filled out and meadows flourished: 'We had this opportunity to manage the land differently, and to be a much smaller cog in a much bigger wheel. Contributing to an environment that you're managing for biodiversity was really important.'

In many ways, the garden comes full circle to his earliest work. Dan grew up in Hampshire and trained at RHS Wisley and Edinburgh's Royal Botanic Garden, before going to the Royal Botanic Gardens, Kew, but the seeds for his future career were sown long before this, by a succession of horticultural mentors. There was his friend and neighbour Geraldine, a naturalist with a wild garden full of plants she had observed and collected on

'I'M CONSTANTLY LEARNING THROUGH THIS PLACE. AND CONSTANTLY TRYING TO PUSH MY OWN BOUNDARIES.'

her travels. Another local, Mrs Pumphrey, had an immaculately maintained and beautiful garden where he worked at weekends and learnt about colour and composition. And then there was the entirely overgrown one-acre garden he tamed over many years with his parents, revealing forgotten treasures that were battling it out with the encroaching wilderness: 'It became my world,' says Dan. Growing up, he says, he was 'a myopic child' and very early on he realised he wanted to make places with plants.

He discovered Beth Chatto, who was also looking to wild settings and putting together plants inspired by their natural habitats. At the same time the naturalistic planting movement was gaining momentum in the Netherlands and Germany.

When he was 18 and still studying at Wisley, he gained his first client – Frances Mossman. A friend of his mother, Frances would later buy the 18th-century Home Farm in Northamptonshire where Dan started to develop the idea of gardening with no boundaries in a four-acre garden, inspired in part by the natural wildflower communities of plants that he was seeing during a one-year scholarship at the Jerusalem Botanic Gardens. The project, which he worked on for 12 years, became a TV series and a book and, in many ways, the precursor to Hillside.

A singular focus ripples through his gardens, which are characterised by exceptional plantsmanship, an innate sensitivity to the natural world and an uncompromising approach to design that somehow never feels overbaked. All qualities that are exemplified in projects such as the epic Tokachi Millennium Forest in Hokkaido, a landscape designed to be sustainable for 1,000 years, or his reimagining of ancient ruins at the hilltop castle, Torrecchia Vecchia, a 1,500-acre estate in Lazio, Italy, and at Lowther Castle in Cumbria.

Pearson's cerebral approach to his craft is crystallised through the written word, too – a habit an English teacher encouraged at school and which has continued throughout his career via numerous books, a decade as gardening columnist at the *Observer* (which he describes as 'a golden ten years') and, since 2016, in his weekly newsletter Dig Delve, which is an eclectic collection of deep dives into plants, design and developments at Hillside.

Yet there's no sense that he sits on his laurels; if anything, his own garden is where he pushes forward with experimentation and investigation. 'I'm constantly learning through this place,' he agrees. 'And constantly trying to push my own boundaries.'

The sand garden is the current focus in this quest. Inspired in part by Peter Korn's experiments into planting into sand, the new area also nods to Dan's work on the Delos garden of Mediterranean plants at Sissinghurst, where weathered stone and architectural fragments create the backdrop to a reimagining of Vita Sackville-West's Greek-inspired garden, originally built in the 1950s. Here there are yew domes providing some grounding structure and antique stone mortars – sourced from a collector of Japanese artefacts – that act as small reflective pools to neighbouring feathery *Stipa* and the velvet spires of *Salvia sclarea* 'Vatican White'. 'The sky is big here and it's nice to bring it down into the water,' explains Dan.

The expansive planting areas (bordered above by a beautiful dry Cotswold stone wall and banks with what will eventually be a shade garden) are cut through with a simple curving path made in local reclaimed Victorian brick. There are plants that thrive on sun-baked Mediterranean hills – *Phlomis italica, Bupleurum longifolium* and *Cistus*, as well as silvery plants such as *Verbascum, Ballota, Onopordum myriacanthum* and *Convolvulus cneorum*. Bulbs, including *Gladiolus tristis* and *Eremurus*, bring colour later in the season.

For Dan, who researched the plant palette at Olivier Filippi's nursery in the south of France, one eye here is on future projects. He had already played with planting into gravelly rubble here around the barns, where pioneering plants would self-seed around less overzealous species (this seemingly wild corner is also the most intensively cultivated patch of the whole plot). The sand garden serves as a test bed for the plants that can withstand the effects of climate change – which can mean prolonged drought in summer, coupled with increasingly wet winters. Young plants start out here in 20 cm (8 inches) of sand, which helps keep the winter wet away from their necks, but also conserves moisture in the richer soil lower down for the dry periods.

There is constant cross-pollination between Hillside and Dan's design practice. On the other side of the plot, next to a large pond that was added in 2021, a building constructed in hardwood recycled from dock groins, with Douglas fir and a cedar shingle roof, was inspired by his many trips to Japan. Down at this perpetually damp end of the garden, it feels like a very different, watery world. Wetland wildflowers sweep around the margins of the pond, where he hopes fritillaries will one day flourish. Thousands of snowdrops have been added to make a snowdrop trail, lighting up the meadow edges in winter (these are kept away from a more selective collection closer to the house), and are often planted with friends or studio colleagues on winter days. In summer this area lights up with the creamy white flowers of *Rosa soulieana,* with its silvery foliage picking up on shimmering leaves of surrounding poplars and nearby *Salix purpurea* 'Nancy Saunders'.

Increasingly, it's these less intensively managed areas that hold Dan's attention most. 'If I ever run out of energy, I'd probably take the garden away or find a way of gardening with trees with grass and bulbs', he says as he walks back up across the wildflower meadow that surrounds the pond. 'It's very easy to say that, but it's so fascinating – it's different every year.'

HARRY AND DAVID RICH

POWYS

When Harry Rich relocated to the secluded cottage just north of the Bannau Brycheiniog (formerly the Brecon Beacons) in Wales where he now lives with his wife Sue and their two children, it was perhaps inevitable that he would create a garden with his younger brother, David.

The siblings first hit public consciousness as the youngest winners of a gold medal at the Chelsea Flower Show in 2012, when Harry had just formed his landscape architecture firm and David was still at university. After graduating, they joined forces as a studio, creating two more gardens at Chelsea and a succession of private and public projects, including gardens for Chanel, Studioilse and Heckfield Place in Hampshire. But this is their most personal project – a mesmerising and magical garden immersed in an ancient landscape of hawthorn, hazel, willow, holly and alder, close to where they grew up.

Harry hadn't even got as far as the house when he knew it was *the one* back in December 2017. Reached via a rugged common and a descent down a precarious narrow track, the house is only accessible by bridge over a picturesque brook, a tributary of the River Wye, that runs the length of the property. The dense shelter here means that in the still of winter the sun barely peeks through the surrounding trees, turning the whole plot into a huge frost pocket for months on end. The brothers soon realised that adding significant structure to the garden was key.

They began by pulling back the land around the house, cutting into the wild banks at the rear of the property to allow the house to breathe. They repositioned dry stone walls to create a more logical approach to the house, marking out defined boundaries but also connecting the house to stone steps that lead down to the brook. Removing an old lean-to also liberated an area for a small terrace with table and chairs to catch the evening light that floods the garden.

The principal forms here come from yew; young hedging demarcates each area of the one-acre garden and is already starting to have a presence around the borders to the front of the house. There are loosely shaped yew domes that punctuate the cultivated garden, while a secluded courtyard on the east-facing side of the house has large yew cubes surrounding multistem *Malus* 'Evereste' that are underplanted with peonies and *Geranium nodosum*. The lush leaves of *Magnolia sieboldii* add to the contrasts of greens.

A run of pleached crab apples cuts across the main beds, marking the spot where the original part of the house meets more recent additions; in spring, the trees provide a cloud of blossom, but by midsummer the structure frames views across the planting below.

The main event for now are these deep and immersive herbaceous borders that spill out across the front of the house. Clumps of statuesque *Eupatorium* tower above a blur of spires and soft umbels in an exquisite palette of pale yellow, cream, white and the burnished tones of earlier flowering plants such as *Sanguisorba* that have already gone over. Golden *Digitalis ferruginea* 'Gigantea' sits alongside *Selinum wallichianum*, *Verbascum chaixii* 'Album' and *Rosa* 'Lichfield Angel'. *Thalictrum* varieties emerge through the season, including 'Black Stockings', 'Elin' and then 'Splendide White'. Pops of yellow come from

'MAKING THE GARDEN, WE'VE LEARNT MORE ABOUT WHO WE ARE AS DESIGNERS.'

fennel, wafts of *Scabiosa ochroleuca* or the beautifully scented *Nepeta govaniana*. Dotted through are clumps of *Doellingeria umbellata* and softening grasses, including *Molinia* 'Transparent'.

The whole effect is elegantly understated, with just an occasional jolt of colour from a vivid red *Hemerocallis* or *Echinops bannaticus* 'Taplow Blue'. Earlier in the season there are Sibirica irises (including 'Papillon' and 'Perry's Blue'). Wild self-seeders including *Achillea* and ribwort plantain are welcomed along the edges of narrow paths.

On a west-facing lime-rendered wall, *Rosa* 'Cécile Brünner' is trained across a lattice of sturdy hazel poles, while at the far end of the house *R.* 'Paul's Himalayan Musk' has already scrambled up to first-floor windows. *R. spinosissima* 'Falkland' has recently been planted and will in time begin to arch over a low stone wall. 'Every day, I get to observe the plants here,' says Harry. 'They are quite large beds but I could put in all my favourite things and play around with combinations, seeing how they grow. Making the garden, we've learnt more about who we are as designers.'

When they arrived, there was little here to keep and the garden was mostly laid to lawn, but there were a few treasures, including a mature *Hamamelis x intermedia* 'Jelena'. They decided to relocate it to the corner of the herbaceous borders, where it arches gracefully over steps down to the stream and is underplanted with a lush carpet of geraniums. 'We'd never moved a mature tree and we knew it was a risk, but it was originally sitting on stone and has thrived since being replanted,' says David.

In 2020, when they began to put in the first plants, they added lots of new topsoil to the borders, although the existing soil is moist but free-draining thanks to the stony ground. In winter, along with a *Chimonanthus praecox* by the door, the graceful witch hazel brings precious scent and colour. Another keeper was a mature *Ribes sanguineum* which hangs over the entrance path and provides vivid pink blooms in spring.

Throughout the garden, Harry and David have made subtle connections with the surrounding landscape, choosing trees that link with the species populating the woods and common, including *Malus sylvestris*, hawthorns and hazel, so that the garden is ornamental but still very much in touch with its environment. Through spring, wilder forms of bulbs also feel appropriate to the setting, with snowdrops, *Tulipa sylvestris* and narcissi planted into the borders. Rather than waging war against regular garden pests such as slugs or rabbits, the principal nuisance here are sheep. One morning Harry woke up to a flock of 40 or 50 who were happily making their way through the borders and had to be ushered out through the narrow gap between the stone walls.

What's abundantly clear in this garden is the degree to which the brothers have literally carved a garden from scratch and clawed back land from the encroaching wilderness. They've done all the work themselves, including building a studio at the far end of the garden where Harry can paint, and they are exceptionally hands-on, which they attribute to their outdoorsy childhood with parents who were equally pragmatic and inventive.

The biggest challenge was access – or lack of – as there are no kerb-side deliveries in this remote and challenging location. Almost all supplies have to be carried down to site, so reusing existing and found materials was paramount. 'Everything was a process and took twice as long,' says David of the initial landscaping. 'We can't just get a delivery here.'

But this has also forced them into working at a slower pace, which in turn has allowed them to wait and observe the land. Their plans have evolved and they are happy to leave elements of the garden – such as some of the hardscaping – undone for now. Among the future plans are a large kitchen garden at the far end of the site where they can have a working kitchen garden, herb garden and greenhouse. And at some point they'd like to cut into the banks more on the north side of the cottage to create some meadow areas and plant fruit trees. 'It doesn't look too polished,' says David, who lives in nearby Brecon. 'We don't have loads of time so it's more on the wild side and we approach it in a relaxed way.'

In many ways, the garden has marked a recalibration of their design practice. After their run of Chelsea wins, they started working in television. It gave them far more exposure as well as a steep learning curve on creating gardens with tiny budgets and really tight turnarounds, building gardens from scratch in just two days. But increasingly it took them away from their own design practice, so after the pandemic they took stock and decided to focus full time on their studio. 'It became a choice between presenting and plants,' recalls Harry. Ten years after their last Chelsea outing, they often ponder a return to creating another show garden too. But for now they are busy with new projects in Wales, Devon, Hampshire and further afield in the Mediterranean, and in their pockets of free time continuing to craft their blissfully secluded garden at home. Despite their high-profile work, this is perhaps where they are happiest. 'We are quite quiet people,' adds Harry. 'We like our personal space.'

SARAH PRICE

MONMOUTHSHIRE

Sarah Price rarely finishes a sentence as we tour her garden on the outskirts of Abergavenny in Monmouthshire; her eyes are constantly darting to a newly emerged planting combination, or a surprise appearance by a particularly distracting self-seeder. 'In the evenings I'll walk around and notice things I've forgotten, or little associations,' she says. 'The garden is a test bed, but it's also like a library or sketchbook that I can draw on for future schemes.'

This close observation of form, colour and composition informs her compelling and influential work; her painterly schemes are rich in atmosphere and complex, naturalistic layering of plants.

Sarah originally studied fine art before taking a job as a gardener at Hampton Court Palace and then pursuing a garden design course. In 2006, she entered and won a Royal Horticultural Society competition to create a design for the Hampton Court Flower Show. This was swiftly followed by two gardens at the Chelsea Flower Show in quick succession, after which she was asked to work as part of the team for the planting design at London's 2012 Olympic Park. It was a dizzying ascent.

But plants had always been part of her life. Growing up, she helped her father on his 'wild' allotment. As one of five siblings it was, she says, a way of spending time with him away from everyone else. Although they lived just outside London, in school holidays she would visit her grandparents' Abergavenny garden, which opened for the National Garden Scheme for decades: 'I had the experience of picking mulberries, or running through an ox-eye daisy meadow. Gardening was highly valued in my household.' In 2013, she moved back to her grandparents' property with her husband Jack and their two children.

On the site of a walled kitchen garden (originally one of two productive gardens here), she has made a beguiling gravel garden. It thrums with life and movement as bees, hoverflies and butterflies dance around the luminous planting, which combines drought-tolerant perennials, biennials and annuals; there are salvias, geraniums, sedums, *Calamintha nepeta* 'Blue Cloud' and billowy swathes of *Scabiosa ochroleuca* 'Moon Dance', as well as Mediterranean shrubs and sub-shrubs such as *Cistus* x *argenteus* 'Silver Pink', *Santolina* or *Lotus hirsutus*. Tucked in among them she trials plants such as the drough-resistant lilac-flowered *Kalimeris*.

The largely purple, blue and white palette of plants is contrasted with the zingy acid of *E. seguieriana subsp. niciciana* – along with *E. rigida*, it's one of eight different euphorbias in the garden – that retains its shape for months on end, flowering until November. 'In a normal border with higher nutrients it would flop everywhere,' says Sarah. The careful orchestration of year-round structure, including silvery sea kales that are dotted about, underpins more ephemeral planting.

There's also an emphasis on plants with a really long season, such as *Oenothera stricta* 'Sulphurea' which will flower until the first frosts: 'It looks horrible if you put it in a conventional border, it needs heat and space.' Needless to say it looks exquisite here, rising up among dark salvias or behind rich purple *Origanum laevigatum* 'Herrenhausen'. In spring, elegant species bulbs including *Tulipa turkestanica*, *T. humilis* 'Persian Pearl' and *T. bakeri* 'Lilac Wonder' bring early colour.

'THE GARDEN IS A TEST BED, BUT IT'S ALSO LIKE A LIBRARY OR SKETCHBOOK THAT I CAN DRAW ON FOR FUTURE SCHEMES.'

Originally, Sarah planted into the existing soil, but the high annual seed content meant that it was impossible to gain an upper hand. So she stripped the soil away and replaced it with three different sizes of recycled sand and gravel. 'I'd heard about Peter Korn's experiments with sand and I just thought I'd try recycled materials,' she explains. 'It's all about how the plant community interacts.' The lower nutrients result in shorter plants and more intricately knitted combinations, and because they are grown hard there is no need for staking or watering.

Numerous grasses, including *Pennisetum macrourum, Melica ciliata, Seslaria nitida, Stipa splendens* as well as *Poa* and *Briza*, also add to the underlying structure and bring a diaphanous layer of texture and movement. Self-seeders keep the planting dynamic but also provide more stock (instead of collecting seed, Sarah lets things seed in the path and then pots them up). And golden seedheads also play an important part, adding structure and contrast through late summer and autumn.

Although aesthetically distinct, it's impossible not to trace the threads of influence from this space to her incomparable design for the 2023 Chelsea Flower Show, which was inspired by the paintings and plants of the artist Cedric Morris and his garden at Benton End in Suffolk. There are the subtle but rich plant pairings and the pink-painted walls that remain behind the original Victorian greenhouse here; there are dark and glossy *Aeoniums* and glaucous *Cotyledons,* too – planted here in rubble-filled Victorian cold frames. Humble benches and stools are crafted from fallen wood and experimental air-dried pots made from reclaimed waste materials provide what Sarah describes as 'intentional garden moments' around the space. This is inventive, resourceful and deeply creative gardening.

It also doesn't stand still. The original Victorian greenhouse has just been taken down after many years of repair jobs and will be rebuilt, keeping the proportions of the original greenhouse but on a smaller footprint that will also allow space for an area to sit and work. 'It's important to have these spaces or clearances, reminding you that you are not in a nature reserve, even if a garden can be richer than a nature reserve,' she explains of the careful balance of a garden so focused on wildlife. 'Often what gives an atmosphere is the biodiversity because it makes the garden feel comfortable and alive, and you feel part of something when you are immersed within the plants. It's something we've all become dissociated from. The movement, the sound – it's really deep.'

But this is very much a garden of two halves, and through a tunnel visitors emerge into a secret orchard meadow bordered on one side with mature ash, hazel, hawthorn, birch and oak trees and on the other with the Cibi river, where grazing cattle come to drink. Originally covered in brambles, they began to clear this patch of land 20 years ago and kept attacking it over time. A group of semi-dwarf apple trees selected by her late father and planted by Sarah now bring beautiful form and colour to the centre of the space.

She added *Deschampsia cespitosa* and then asters, *Thalictrum, Sanguisorba* and *Paeonia mascula*, which had orginally been planted by her grandmother in another area of the garden. A succession of geraniums, including the magenta 'Catherine Deneuve', bring colour throughout the season. They've topiarised self-seeded oak and beech trees, which add intriguing forms, acting as anchor points in the haze of plants. 'I don't like the hand of the gardener to be evident,' she says. 'But you do have to go in and edit for it not to be messy.' Plants here tend to be as close to the species as possible, such as *Rosa* 'Partridge', which she says is a useful groundcover but will also scramble up over walls too. They've recently added a pool and commissioned local artist Mick Petts to craft an arching bridge using a fallen wych elm.

Back through the tunnel there are more pockets of delicious planting; two roses – *Rosa* 'Bengal Crimson' and *R.* x *odorata* 'Mutabilis' entwine beside a wall underplanted with loose, elegant annuals, including the pale apricot *Scabiosa atropurpurea* 'Fata Morgana'.

Around the corner, you are suddenly immersed in another mood shift – a glorious lush and shady seating areas circled with ferns, small-leaved azaleas and cloud-pruned *Acer campestre*. In spring and early summer, the ground is covered with anemones and corydalis. A textural waterbowl reflects the glossy green leaves of an osmanthus above. All around there are shrubs originally planted by her grandmother – a fuchsia in palest pink, a gloriously vibrant *Hydrangea aspera*. And next to it all, the river rushes noisily down from the Black Mountains, adding yet another dimension to this otherworldly garden.

NIGEL DUNNETT

SOUTH YORKSHIRE

Nigel Dunnett's garden, which sits on the edge of the Peak District, just west of Sheffield, would be described by almost any gardener as challenging. Built on a steep north-facing slope on the site of an old quarry, it spans just over an acre with stony, shallow soil. 'A lot of the early years,' he recalls, 'were spent trying to make things accessible and usable.' Over the past decade he has carved out distinct zones, each with its own character, joined by a series of informal timber paths and steps, that tread the fine line between cultivated and wild.

The garden reflects the many facets of his work as Professor of Planting Design and Urban Horticulture at Sheffield University. There are no traditional beds or borders here, instead there is an immersive haze of vegetation: 'My philosophy is: if it lives and survives, then plant more. If it doesn't, I'm not going to spend any time trying to make it.'

Close to the house that he shares with his wife, Marta, the feeling is more cultivated. Nigel points to one perfectly pitched small area – a garden in microcosm with *Geum* 'Lemon Drops', *Carex elata* 'Aurea', melica, geraniums and lady ferns. Earlier in the season, hellebores and snowdrops flower, while later eupatoriums will rise up through the dense foliage. It's a perfect illustration of his approach, bringing together plant communities that will provide almost year-round interest, with minimal intervention.

This hands-off approach is echoed throughout. At the front of the house, a rain garden is a working example of his landscape research, capturing and then diverting water into planting areas, or 'bioswales', either side of a path with a carefully calibrated succession of layers. Spring primulas, polyanthus and buttercups are followed by *Iris sibirica*, *Geranium sylvaticum*, day lilies, *Astilbe* 'Purplelanz', rudbeckias and *Crocosmia* 'Solfatare'. Towering over it all is *Miscanthus* x *giganteus* which reaches almost three metres (10 feet) in height by late summer. 'It's a really important principle for me in a small space to not use dwarf plants, but to use big plants,' he says of the dramatic way he has transformed a tricky triangular patch of land into a relatively low-maintenance tapestry of texture, form and colour.

One of the most distinctive (and much copied) elements are the sinuous log piles that are repeated across the garden. When Nigel first started clearing the site, he removed sycamore trees to create more space for the oaks at the top of the plot and began using the logs as a decorative element. Their undulating forms echo the dry stone walls of the Peak District hills. They were also inspired, he says, by Piet Oudolf's garden at Hummelo, where layers of curving hedges play off against each other as you move around them. In summer, the logs largely disappear from view as they are submerged in planting, but in winter they are vital structure, and also provide habitat for insects, invertebrates and other small creatures.

In many ways, he is simply designing with what is close at hand; woody stems and prunings have been made into a dead hedge 'nest' high up in the garden – a really effective sculptural feature with huge wildlife benefits, too. Above this a woodland area is informally circled by self-seeded elders and beyond them native hollies, birch, elder and oaks. A circle of logs demarcates an area treated as a meadow with spring bulbs emerging early in

'MY PHILOSOPHY IS: IF IT LIVES AND SURVIVES, THEN PLANT MORE. IF IT DOESN'T, I'M NOT GOING TO SPEND ANY TIME TRYING TO MAKE IT.'

the season. 'I think it would be sacrilegious to start trying to plant stuff into it and make a garden. It's just very special like it is.'

Nigel was entranced by nature from an early age when he explored bluebell woods and meadows in Kent where he grew up, but he soon realised he never got the same joyful feelings when he was in a cultivated garden. 'I just started wondering why that was and that got me just looking at small patches of plants in my parents' garden and doing similar things.' He went on to study botany at university, rationalising that he could teach himself anything else he needed to know about design or horticulture but couldn't teach himself science and ecology.

Through his projects, from the Barbican Estate in the City of London to the hugely successful urban greening of Sheffield over the past two decades, he has been at the forefront of the naturalistic planting movement and bringing a 'people first' approach, in which the visual effects of his schemes are as important as the biodiversity and ecological benefits.

Perhaps he is best-known for vibrant perennial meadows, not least because they've appeared in some of his most high-profile projects, including London's Olympic Park in 2012, and at the Queen's Jubilee in 2022 when he filled the 14,000-m^2 (151,000-ft^2), 13th-century moat of the Tower of London with flowers.

The driest area of his garden, by a Swedish yellow shed, has been given over to grids of meadow, clumps of blue oat grass (*Helicotrichon sempervirens*) and *Kniphofia*, surrounded by a yellow and orange mix with *Calendula officinalis* 'Orange King', *Chrysanthemum carinatum* 'Flame Shades', *Coreopsis tinctoria* 'Dwarf Mix', *Eschscholzia californica* 'Golden West', *Rudbeckia hirta* 'My Joy', *Tagetes* 'Lemon Gem' and a smattering of blue from *Centaurea cyanus* 'Blue Boy'. In another area, he has sown a cosmos-heavy mix of pastel shades, including Shirley poppies, cosmos, cornflowers, *Ammi majus* and *Gypsophila elegans* 'Covent Garden'.

Pictorial Meadows – in which he designs mixes of both annual and perennial meadow seed mixes that are sold commercially – began life on his kitchen table, but has since been sold and is now run by a social enterprise in Sheffield. 'I knew that the meadows would have this kind of magnetic effect on people. But I had no idea that they'd be used in such a big way.'

Nigel's inclination to experiment and to create visual effects is evident through his own garden, too. One of the first areas he planted at home was a copse of paper birch with beautiful peeling copper bark. Inspired by old landscape gardening techniques, detailed by Humphry Repton, where young bare root trees are planted together in the same hole, he planted three saplings together. Twelve years on, there are more dominant plants surrounded by smaller trees. Higher up the hill he used a similar method to plant an avenue of *Sorbus aucuparia*, which now tower over head, providing white flowers in spring, intense orange fruits in summer and beautiful structure in winter.

Thanks to the jungle of densely packed plants, there's little chance of getting in to do any maintenance in most areas here beyond May. But this is perhaps a blessing. When he was first shaping the garden and attempting to tame this patch of land into some kind of rational scheme, he didn't really consider any time to enjoy the garden. 'I was spending all hours just climbing my way into this and Marta said, "Well, you know, you can't spend all your time just working. The gardens are to rest and relax and to sit in".' Now visitors find a plethora of chairs, arranged up and down this transporting garden – although it's hard to imagine Nigel sitting in one for too long.

SHEILA JACK

WILTSHIRE

As a landscape designer often working on city projects, Sheila Jack's Wiltshire bolthole flipped her practice on its head. Rather than creating views within an urban garden, she was faced with rural vistas in all directions, and a challenging sloping quarter-acre site that had been under concrete for at least half a century. But after converting her former semi-derelict barn – bought at auction with her husband, Paul Barnes – into an elegant, contemporary larch-clad home with James Grayley Architects, the design for the garden came surprisingly easily.

The situation of the garden was paramount. 'It's a beautiful setting and you want to max that out,' says Sheila of the almost 360-degree views across undulating fields and to the River Nadder. Beyond the meadows that are cut for hay, there is distant woodland and the property sits on a dead-end road. During summer evenings resident barn owls swoop across the surrounding land.

Her design focuses on views out from the rooms of the house, with almost every oak-framed window pointing to these stunning vistas, but also to her restrained naturalistic planting. A series of beds, each edged in steel, has a successional matrix of ornamental grasses and pollinator-friendly perennials providing a long season of interest, peaking in late summer and early autumn. *Cephalaria gigantea*, *Nepeta* 'Romany Dusk', *Selinum wallichianum*, *Veronicastrum album* and *Helenium* 'Moerheim Beauty' contrast with spiky *Eryngium yuccifolium* and multiple grasses, including *Molinia* 'Transparent', *Pennisetum* 'Red Head' and *Calamagrostis brachytricha*.

To impose a sense of order on this awkward site, the beds are arranged to reflect the sections of the building, with strong lines reaching out from the bays of the house. Cutting across these lines, a longer curving path leads down to another key element within the landscape – a stunning ancient oak tree beyond the garden's boundary that provides a focal point to the garden's central axis.

One of the biggest challenges of the site was this unprepossessing far end of the garden – a former dumping ground for the farmer and now the location of a septic tank. But it was also potentially a prime spot to sit in the early evening with views to the west. It was, says Sheila, hard to imagine anything growing in the very poor ground. So she devised a run of tough wild roses (including *Rosa canina, R. rubiginosa, R. rugosa and R. moyesii* 'Geranium') that would merge to create a thicket. In front of them there are clipped mounds of *Lonicera nitida*, along with *Rosa glauca*, *R.* x *odorata* 'Mutabilis' and *R. pimpinellifolia*, with *Molinia* 'Moorhexe' contributing some late-season colour and texture. A multistem *Crataegus coccinea* adds a vertical counterpoint, while espalier pear and plum trees provide an additional layer of seasonal interest closer to the house.

Putting together plants that were not 'too gardeny' or too cultivated was a key consideration in a space so immersed in landscape. 'Some things just don't feel right. There are mostly open flowers here, and nothing too ornamental as it feels wrong in this setting,' she says. 'Doubt does creep in when it's your own project and you're thinking "Is that a good fit? Is it too pretentious?"'

Landscape design is a second career for Sheila, a former graphic designer who worked first for the American edition of *Vogue* and then later at *Harper's Bazaar* where she was art director.

‘I’VE SPENT A LIFETIME LOOKING AND MAKING AESTHETIC JUDGEMENTS, A LIFETIME LOOKING AT COMPOSITION.’

After creating an elegant white garden at her West London house, she retrained at the London College of Garden Design, Kew. ‘It was exciting to be learning something new. It was so invigorating,’ she recalls. She won the 2021 Society of Garden Designers’ Fresh Designer Award for an early project – a contemporary meadow garden in Brixton, South London. In 2024 she was named one of *House & Garden*’s top 50 garden designers.

Her decades of experience in creating sleek layouts for magazines undoubtedly play out in her rigorous designs, which balance a strong spatial awareness with joyful, elegant planting. And there are many parallels between the two disciplines: ‘I’ve spent a lifetime looking and making aesthetic judgements, a lifetime looking at composition.’ All that experience is poured into her gardens with their uncompromising approach to form and materials – unsurprisingly, her favourite projects are where she works closely with architects and interior designers. And it’s strongly in evidence in her Wiltshire garden.

Despite its contemporary design, nothing feels out of place here. To ensure that the new garden connected with the surrounding landscape around the other boundaries, she planted sections of yew hedging that will eventually be cloud-pruned but still kept low. Trees are carefully selected; in a gently stepped lawn, two borders are studded with multistem *Malus* ‘Evereste’, in a nod to an orchard that was once planted here. Beneath them, some clipped *Taxus* domes, are contrasted with swathes of *Sesleria autumnalis* and layers of bulbs, including narcissi, iris, alliums and the rare and particularly beautiful *Camassia leitchlinii* ‘Pink Star’.

To the left, a small meadow and hornbeam hedging separate the utilitarian parking area from the main garden. This subtle boundary also helps create seclusion and privacy. Materials were sourced as locally as possible; a series of small terraces and paths are paved in Purbeck stone pitchers, which also form the steps in the lawn. Boulders in Chilmark stone dotted through the garden come from a nearby quarry and gravel was sourced locally, too. Concrete that was removed from the original yard was reused in gabion walls.

Close to the house, a galvanised steel tank – which has been treated to create a lead-like patina and painted black inside – provides mesmerising reflections of the surrounding trees, including those crab apples and the farmland oak tree, as well as delicate perennial planting which includes *Echinacea pallida* and allium seedheads. It’s one of the most successful details in a garden full of ideas to steal.

CHRIS MOSS

WEST SUSSEX

Framing the views is given new meaning at Chris Moss's picturesque, tile-hung cottage that sits on the edge of the Leconfield Estates and the South Downs National Park in West Sussex. In 2019, when he first arrived, the mid-18th century home had been recently renovated, but as a listed building with small windows, creating verdant vistas directly from each window became paramount – 'I wanted it to feel as though you could just reach out and touch the plants,' says the designer.

Throughout the borders at the front and back of the house the feeling is billowy and light. At the front, four beds, arranged either side of a simple winding brick path, are woven with airy plants that are exquisitely pretty but entirely distinct from formulaic cottage-garden schemes – the only nod to it a couple of old roses, thought to have been planted around time of the Second World War, that have been retained.

In late summer there's a haze of Japanese anemones (including 'Prinz Heinrich', 'Königin Charlotte' and 'Honorine Jobert') and the tall white daisy, *Erigeron annuus*, which readily self-seeds and flowers for many months. Towering above them is the pretty *Althaea cannabina* – a mallow with clouds of delicate, clear pink flowers and growing to over two metres (eight feet) tall in the garden's damp clay soil. 'Everything comes up to eye level so the cottage looks smaller,' explains Chris. 'I wanted people to feel completely absorbed by it, so that the plants take over.'

There are clumps of *Symphyotrichum* 'Little Carlow' (a favourite for its easy growth habit and resistance to mildew), and dotted throughout is the annual *Ammi majus*, added late in the season to flower through August and into early autumn. Along the path, *Origanum laevigatum 'Herrenhausen'* adds a pop of intense purple.

Chris rents the cottage from a long-standing client who lives nearby and this was an additional consideration in the design: 'I couldn't just fill it full of plants. I had to have quite contained beds, because one day I might not be here, and they could keep the perennials here and work with them.' Nonetheless, he's been given free rein to create the garden – the only request was not to use yellow; standing out in the haze of delicate pinks, blue and whites is an errant yellow self-seeded *Verbascum*.

Despite growing up in a family of gardeners in Lancashire, becoming a designer didn't occur to Chris until he was studying at the Sorbonne in Paris and visiting grand gardens such as Fontainebleau and Versailles. On a visit to the latter, he saw there was a course in garden design and it sparked an interest. Back at home, the designer Robin Williams advised him to first learn how to build gardens, so he went to work for landscape specialist Mark Gregory. At the same time, he studied horticulture and garden design at Merrist Wood College. He went on to work with Fiona Lawrenson for eight years, before setting up his own studio in 2004.

When he started the garden here, Chris began with two smaller beds with native wild flowers using plugs, but space has gradually been given over to more cultivated plants. *Knautia*, *Achillea*, plantains and ox-eye daisies now grow alongside perennials, including *Sanguisorba* and *Agastache foeniculum* 'Alabaster', *Selinum wallichianum* and *Verbena hastata rosea*.

‘I DON’T EVER WANT A GARDEN TO FEEL TOO DESIGNED… IT SHOULD FEEL LIKE IT’S ALWAYS BEEN HERE.’

Fennel, dill and lovage are also dotted through, as well as *Calamintha nepeta* ‘Blue Cloud’, which he often uses in clients’ gardens alongside catmint for succession.

In contrast to all of the light and breezy planting, Chris has incorporated strong structure. He enclosed the front garden with beech hedging, which he has started to gently cloud prune, and a collection of clipped trees and shrubs bring year-round presence and frame the front of the cottage. A large-leaved hawthorn, *Crataegus coccinea*, almost reaching the eaves of the cottage, sits in one border with pretty blush berries in summer. Closer to the front of the garden there’s a topiarised multistem beech. Dotted throughout the space are *Osmanthus* x *burkwoodii*, clipped into domes of different sizes, their white blossom providing a layer of interest above a sea of snowdrops, hellebores and tulips in spring.

The back garden leads straight into woodland so it was important to maintain the views out and keep the design simple – a central path leads straight to a cleft chestnut post-and-rail fence and wooden gate. In place of solid boundary fencing, Chris has used a mixed native hedge – beloved by the abundant local birdlife here, which includes nightingales – and hazel hurdles along one side of the garden. Three multistem hornbeam trees are dotted through the garden to bring some structure but are loosely pruned so that they don’t look too formal.

On the opposite side of the garden, his neighbours removed a section of their boundary, so he has entirely replanted this corner. There’s a *Malus* ‘Evereste’ tree underplanted with lush foliage plants including *Euphorbia* x *pasteurii*, *Rodgersia* and *Dryopteris erythrosora,* providing rich bronze foliage in autumn. Close by, banks of *Persicaria amplexicaulis* ‘Fat Domino’ provide vivid red flowers right outside one of the kitchen windows, while the single hybrid tea rose ‘Mrs Oakley Fisher’ has single apricot blooms and hips later in the season. A Hungarian cattle trough is filled with water for passing birds and insects.

The terrace, paved in reclaimed York stone slabs, is dotted with beautifully choreographed pots featuring *Oenothera lindheimeri, Salvia* ‘Nachtvlinder’, *Verbena officinalis* ‘Bampton’ and *Scabiosa incisa* ‘Kudo Blue’. Perennials from the borders, including *Scabiosa ochrolecua* and *Calamintha nepeta,* happily self-seed into cracks in the paving.

The back garden borders are perhaps a little wilder but more subdued than the front, harmonising with the woodland behind. There are *Sanguisorba* ‘Red Thunder’ and ‘Cangshan Cranberry’, *Succisella inflexa* ‘Frosted Pearls’ and swathes of the delicate *Heuchera villosa*, with spires of creamy flowers and beautiful foliage, which Chris discovered on a trip to Vitra, a Piet Oudolf garden in Weil am Rhein in Germany.

Different forms of *Molinia*, including ‘Heidebraut’, ‘Transparent’, and in the front garden the beautiful dark form ‘Black Arrows’, bring texture and movement without being too dominant: ‘I like the fact that you see through them, like a gauze.’ Mounds of evergreen *Carex secta* provide structure through to late winter, when it’s pruned just as the garden is full of primroses which seed from the local woodland – cultivated bulbs tend to look too brash so close to the wildflowers.

At the far end of the plot, the newest addition to the garden is a timber potting shed, complete with a peg-tiled roof and nestled into the chestnut fence. For Chris, whose projects tend to be on old properties and using local materials and skilled craftsman, creating these kinds of harmonious vignettes is second nature. ‘I don’t ever want a garden to feel too designed,’ he says. ‘It should feel like it’s always been here.’

ARNE MAYNARD

MONMOUTHSHIRE

When Arne Maynard moved to Allt y bela, the medieval house's unrelenting asymmetry proved to be something of a stumbling block, albeit a temporary one. Along with his partner William Collinson, he had moved from Guanock House on the flat, wind-swept plains of The Fens in Lincolnshire, where he'd spent a decade creating a garden of strong axes, formal borders and immaculate symmetry, to the rolling hills and verdant valleys of Monmouthshire. The contrasts of climate, topography and architecture could not have been more dramatic.

Allt y bela was built as a cruck-frame hall house in the mid-15th century. An additional floor was later added, followed by the distinctive tower in 1599. When the couple arrived in 2005, the house was entirely surrounded by trees. 'You couldn't see out at all,' says the designer. 'I just wanted it to be part of the landscape and for the garden to flow.' After a year of observation they began to remove trees, walls, gates and railings, reconnecting the building to its bucolic setting.

Arne's gardens, such as those at Haddon Hall in Derbyshire or South Wood Farm in Devon, are renowned for their deft combination of formality with soft, luxuriant planting, exquisitely crafted details and a deep sense of place. Perhaps more than anything, he's known for his use of topiary, often inspired by the meticulously clipped shapes in the gardens of storied Elizabethan houses such as Levens Hall in Cumbria or Beckley Park in Oxfordshire.

'One of the things that I was struggling with at Allt y bela was that the house is so tall. It's like a skyrocket that just shoots up. It was really dominant.' Arne bought around 40 yew bushes and started to plant them out. 'I just placed them anywhere I felt we needed to have scale and weight.' And while at first, he says, it looked like a Christmas tree farm, it's the mature topiary that now defines this garden. Along with the yew, box and beech are clipped into neat balls, domes, lollipops or layered cones in various heights that cluster around buildings, paths and cross-points, anchoring the house and vertiginous tower, and punctuating borders. In the winter, when the garden 'shrinks', the collection of topiary pieces, including a copper beech spiral, come into their own.

Another early move was to plant a run of espalier *Malus* 'Evereste' along the front of the house, enclosing an area that the designer refers to as his 'cabinet of curiosities', where favourite roses such as 'Cardinal de Richelieu' and historic tulips grow alongside more neatly clipped topiary.

Arne describes himself as foremost a gardener who designs. While not horticulturally trained, growing up in rural Dorset he gardened from early childhood, mentored by the brilliant plantsmen and women around him, and a prescient godmother took him to visit gardens. His design awakening came from a neighbour, Mrs Ordish, who would regale him with her planting approach – adding a swathe of 'China Town' tulips underneath a Bramley apple tree so that they would flower in unison with the pretty pink blossom, or planting sweetly scented daphne by the door to enjoy its perfume in the depths of winter – all lessons he has carried into his design work. In his early teens, he also discovered nearby Cranborne Manor, then gardened by Lady Salisbury.

'ONE OF THE THINGS THAT I WAS STRUGGLING WITH AT ALLT Y BELA WAS THAT THE HOUSE IS SO TALL. IT'S LIKE A SKYROCKET THAT JUST SHOOTS UP. IT WAS REALLY DOMINANT.'

After studying architecture, Arne's interest in antique details and craftsmanship was honed at Clifton Little Venice, then owned by Lord Jacob Rothschild, where he worked with the celebrated plaster caster Peter Hone sourcing architectural antiques, a pivotal period he fondly describes as 'a different type of education'. Through it he found his first client, the advertising guru David Abbott and he began to slowly build his design practice.

At Allt y bela borders have developed organically, stretching out from buildings. Beside the studio, built, like almost everything here, in the local red sandstone, low hawthorn hedges define beds with a moody mix of aquilegias, foxgloves, phlox, *Anthriscus sylvestris* 'Ravenswing', *Verbascum phoeniceum* 'Violetta', *Achillea ageratum* and a beautiful dark form of angelica.

In all directions there are picturesque vignettes: an old wooden coldframe, propped open in the cool evening; stone steps populated with self-seeded foxgloves; an old stone trough edged with small ferns, and clusters of pots filled with collections of favourite violas.

Despite the space, the densely cultivated borders are modest and domestic in scale. To the east of the house, Arne indulges his passion for both old roses, such as 'Tuscany Superb' or the Bourbon 'Gypsy Boy', which is trained on coppiced hazel domes in a cottage-style garden, as well as newer cultivars including the hot pink 'Sir Paul Smith', positioned to tumble over a stone wall. In between the roses there are foxgloves, hardy geraniums, dierama, clematis and oriental poppies, as well as the odd beautiful weed such as salsify or ribwort plantain.

Beyond the rose garden, the formal vegetable garden is bordered by cloud-pruned box and protected with a cleft oak fence. Rows of vegetable and salad crops, some set out under glass cloches, are immaculately laid out in oak-edged raised beds. There are step-over apples, loganberries winding across the fence and roses, peonies and sweet peas for cutting, all thriving in the rich, loamy clay soil.

At the back of the house an elliptical border set into a criss-cross pattern of box is planted in cool blues and soft apricots, its curves echoed with mown paths that cut through a meadow studded with more topiary and early Elizabethan pear varieties. Here there are foxgloves, more roses including 'Jude the Obscure' and 'Perle d'Or', *Paeonia* 'Prairie Moon', *Geranium pratense* 'Summer Skies', *Linaria* 'Canon Went' and *Iris* 'Benton Susan', which chimes beautifully with the ochre paint of the house. A cluster of flowering parsnip cuts throught the pastel tones with its intense acid yellow flowers.

Viewed from above, Allt y bela is a garden full of curves. Hidden away at the head of a valley, nestling in a basin surrounded by sloping wildflower meadows and patches of woodland, its garden is delineated by a serpentine river, canalised with beautiful stone walls, that sweeps across the drive and around buildings before making its way back out of the garden. Its curvaceous path is further emphasised by a grassed amphitheatre – the site of summer plays.

Paramount for Arne was to maximise the natural landscape (which is designated as a Site of Special Scientific Interest) so that his gardens would bleed out into sylvan boundaries. Early on he added tens of thousands of wild narcissi and snowdrops – achieving an instant sense of antiquity by naturalising bulbs *en masse* – and planted rambling roses into ancient trees, which have now scrambled up into the tallest branches.

The surrounding pasture segues gently into the garden too, perhaps most perceptibly in the meadows that Arne has nurtured from scrubby land. To the south, one meadow was labouriously cleared of self-seeded sloes and hawthorns and then routinely cut to reduce, and then eradicate, thuggish weeds including brambles and bracken. Yellow rattle was used to weaken the lush grass and allow the wildflowers that already existed in the seedbank to flourish; now the meadow is a sea of orchids, sorrel and *Persicaria bistorta*. Arne has embellished this with bulbs such as *Iris hollandica* 'Autumn Princess' that pick out the golden buttercups across the meadow. Higher up the slope, *Rosa* x *odorata* 'Bengal Crimson' adds a dramatic fountain of colour.

'This is what I like about being able to do my own gardens. You're not pushed into time restraints, where things have to be finished,' says Arne of the continual experimentation in which he adds additional plants such as astrantias or *Trollius* 'Lemon Queen' to the meadow each year. What's very evident in this mesmerising garden is the constant and close attention to detail, the quest to continually refine and edit, add or subtract, something he can achieve by being in his own garden almost every day.

ARABELLA LENNOX-BOYD

LANCASHIRE

When Arabella Lennox-Boyd first arrived at Gresgarth Hall in Lancashire in 1978, little about the house or garden pleased her. 'I was horrified,' she says of the dour sandstone house that was almost entirely surrounded by enormous Portuguese laurel, woodland and garish azaleas. 'It was very grim and quite depressing.' But her husband Mark, who would become the MP for Morecambe and Lonsdale the following year, had other thoughts. 'He has got a very good eye, and said, "this is perfect and this is practical". I just went with it. I can't say with my heart, because at the beginning I didn't really understand it.'

Getting under the skin of a landscape has long been Arabella's *modus operandi*. The revered and prolific designer has worked on more than 800 projects around the globe, from chic city gardens (including luxury hotel Le Bristol in Paris and No 1 Poultry in London) and sprawling country houses (such as the Duke of Westminster's Eaton Hall in Cheshire) to rock-star retreats (Sting's Villa Il Palagio in Tuscany) and palatial estates, including her own Palazzo Parisi – the remote hilltop house in the Sabine hills north of Rome where she grew up immersed in nature.

As a single parent in London during the 1960s, she had to get a job. She had a large garden in St John's Wood and her gardener suggested she should design for others. Realising that she needed to become more professional, she joined the seven-year Landscape Architecture course at Thames Polytechnic. 'I was brought up in a very old-fashioned way, and as a woman I was not expected to do anything, because one just had to marry and be a wife,' she explains. 'Finding that I could learn all about a subject I really loved, that I could start a business and earn my living was a liberation. Being able to converse with people with the same interests was a revelation.'

Her designs are renowned for their classicism, luxuriant planting and romance, but most of all for their intense sense of place. In many ways, Gresgarth is a deeply biographical garden and arguably her greatest achievement – a portrait of her interests and loves. Across 15 acres she has created a landscape with hundreds of trees, meandering paths, grand herbaceous borders, sweeping vistas and exuberant planting all around. The garden is both awe-inspiring and breathtaking in its beauty.

After clearing trees and opening up the area around the house, Arabella began to create a garden that would tease out the elegance of the idiosyncratic architecture. The house is a curious combination of styles; the oldest part – now the kitchen – dates from around 1380. At the start of the 19th century it was remodelled in the Gothic style with a façade that nods to what is believed to be the remains of a pele tower – a fortification used defensively against raiders from Scotland.

She carved out tiered terraces that would ground the house, immersing it right into the green and connecting it to the wider landscape. The levels, joined by a series of steps, are now richly planted with shrubs, herbaceous perennials and favourite roses, including *Rosa* 'Fantin-Latour' and *R.* 'Empress Josephine', while small octagonal lawns break up the hard landscaping. Additional structure is provided by clipped topiary balls, cubes, lollipops and swirls. Along one side, yew buttresses, topped with two love birds, create a castellated effect. Roses, including the creamy

'I'VE BEEN REALLY LUCKY, BECAUSE I'VE DONE EVERYTHING I WANTED TO DO TO CREATE THE GARDEN I LOVE.'

yellow 'Gardenia', scramble around windows and up to the eaves of the house and tumble over walls.

Gresgarth's sense of place is largely defined by water. It brings constant motion by way of the Artle Beck, a tributary of the River Lune, that over centuries has carved its way through the ancient woodland and around the house, snaking off around the estate's late 18th-century mill house (one of three in the area). A key element in understanding the weather here was to remove vegetation around the river, which would in turn help to take away harsh frosts that roll down from the surrounding hills.

The magical setting is enhanced further by the lake. Water enters through three small, circular ponds, ending in the main stretch of water, which flows towards the lower terrace. A rock is placed facing the west so that evening sun can shine on it.

'It was a trauma,' Arabella says, recalling the significant work involved to remodel the smaller body of water that was originally here. 'Because we redid it twice. The first one had an island, and then I realised that I was going to be looking at a weedy island, so I thought, "No, no, that's got to go".' The house now appears to float in the lake. 'I realised the beauty of a reflection. Here in the North West, the light is just so subtle and beautiful – it has a lot of purple in it,' she explains.

She was inspired by many places and gardens, but a key stimulus was Ninfa, the romantic garden south of Rome. 'It was just like walking into paradise,' recalls Arabella of a trip there before she trained in landscape architecture. 'And that feeling I have never forgotten. For me, it is absolute perfection.'

Beside the lake, a large, circular lawn, surrounded by a yew hedge, provides a moment of calm. On one side the wild garden, with shrubs, grasses and herbaceous plants, leads into the damper water garden, marking the far end of the lake.

A major challenge was to tackle the local conditions – which included damp clay soil and fierce winds from the west. Her solution was to plant layer upon layer of hedges as well as shrubs and trees, including oak and walnut trees to provide shelter. A lilac walk was designed to provide another layer of trees bordering the parkland around the garden, but the lilacs were among the many early casualties here, as she grappled with the wind and wet.

To the west of the house a shady path leads to a series of herbaceous borders; the first an enclosed garden with swirling pebble mosaic paths designed by Maggy Howarth, with the family's zodiac signs joined up by swirls and clouds signifying the Milky Way. Box topiary is joined by frothy mounds of pale pink geraniums, asters and roses. Beyond this, the deep herbaceous borders stretch out with perfectly orchestrated swathes of blues, lilacs and pinks; peonies and poppies, phlox and clematis, thalictrum and more asters all flower in succession. At the far end, in another yew enclosure, the palette shifts to soothing whites and creams.

But it's the trees that are perhaps her greatest passion, many planted from seed and now towering above, reaching heights of nine to 12 metres (30 or 40 feet). 'If you're a bit obsessive,' she admits, 'you can't stop collecting.' Her knowledge was honed on plant hunting trips and a period as a trustee of the Royal Botanic Gardens at Kew. 'It's a huge subject, and so interesting. And I had a wonderful connection with the curator there who is still a great friend. He taught me so much.'

When they first arrived at Gresgarth, Arabella kept mature oaks, beech, limes, conifers and a *Davidia* tree which was discovered by accident. But early on, she began to plant magnolias – there are now more than a hundred, which thrive in the climate here – and, along with *Prunus*, *Malus* and *Amelanchier*, provide an incredible show throughout spring. There is a national collection of *Styracaceae*, as well as *Acer* and *Stewartia* trees. Further into the gardens there are *Hamamelis* and *Rhododendron* walks. Exquisite trees are dotted through the formal gardens, too, including the beautiful *Cercidyphyllum japonicum* captured in the lake's reflection. In autumn, the whole garden is ablaze when her collection unleashes its fiery colours.

It's almost inconceivable that there was no initial masterplan created here, as each area of the garden slots together seamlessly. And it's impossible to imagine a moment in the year when Gresgarth is not magical, from the luminous foliage and bulbs emerging in spring through to the depths of winter when frost laces this landscape.

This is gardening on an epic scale. When we meet in midsummer – just as the wildflowers and *Cornus kousa* are lighting up the open banks edging the woodlands – I try to find her in the gardens. She is immersed in some frantic pruning, clad in arm protectors and submerged under an enormous shrub, while a young gardener stands by awaiting instruction. The next day she is off to Italy on holiday, although she will find time for site visits to potential jobs while she is there. She has no intention of stopping her work anytime soon. At Gresgarth, she says, she wanted to create a welcoming and warm garden. 'I'm quite passionate in my friendships and my family, and that's what I feel I needed here,' she says. 'I've been really lucky, because I've done everything I wanted to do to create the garden I love.'

BUTTER WAKEFIELD

LONDON

If there's a star of the show in Butter Wakefield's west London garden then it is, indisputably, the meadow. From the stable door of her colourful, art-filled kitchen, this tapestry of flowers and grasses stretches out, a glorious slice of the country, in the city.

In succession, spring flowers including narcissi, cowslips and *Geranium phaeum* are followed by *Allium* 'Purple Sensation' and 'Purple Rain', red campion, sorrel, knapweed and vetch, creating a haze of pinks and purples, punctuated with the acid yellow flowers of lady's bedstraw or the golden glow of delicate buttercups. 'It captures my heart because it's ever-changing, every year it's different,' says Butter. For later in the season she's added *Verbena bonariensis*, viper's bugloss, *Eupatorium* and ornamental grasses *Molinia* 'Transparent' and 'Heidebraut'. More recently, she has commissioned willow-weaver Jay Davey to create twisted willow ropes that provide an elegant perimeter to the edge of the meadow.

In the centre, a steel water bowl, filled with a few oxygenting plants and gently trickling water, reflects the surrounding flowers but also provides a place for birds and insects to take a drink. Bringing nature in is central to the designer's ethos, and the garden is actively planted to offer early nectar with spring bulbs and climbing shrubs including an ornamental quince, *Chaenomeles speciosa* 'Nivalis', which is trained along the wall and flowers from late January. Feeders hang from trees and one shady corner is left untouched with leaf litter and decaying logs to provide insect habitats.

But this is a garden for relaxation and entertaining, too. A *Trachelospermum jasminoides* climbs across the back of the house, providing intoxicating summer scent, while a *Magnolia grandiflora* tree provides shade over a seating area, with iron benches and a collection of mismatched pots – some handcrafted in Italian terracotta and others collected from various shows and dealers. Here she has also added a beautiful side-return conservatory with a big sash window allowing more views from inside out into the garden.

Either side of the meadow, a brick-edged lawn path gives access to deep borders that are filled with climbing and shrub roses, including 'The Generous Gardener', 'Madame Alfred Carrière', 'Boscobel' and 'Charles de Mills'. The dominant plants here are hydrangeas 'Limelight' and 'Annabelle' that grow huge in the rich clay soil. These are underplanted with a succession of perennials including geums, aquilegias, cephalaria, *Geranium* 'Ann Folkard' and *Nepeta govaniana* – an unusual yellow form of catmint. Uninvited guests – such as a golden hop – are welcomed in if they add to the scene. On the shadier side of the garden a similar mix of shrubs and perennials is joined by ferns, foxgloves, *Acanthus* and more roses underneath an old apple tree. A stone urn is filled with neat succulents and dotted with delicate perennials, including the sprawling *Geranium pyrenaicum* 'Bill Wallis'.

One of her clever ideas was to enclose a hard-working utility area – a small space where she has a potting bench, compost bin and shed – behind trellis panels covered with *Trachelospermum jasminoides*. In front of this, another layer is added with a small bench topped with an antique laundry basket, which is filled with tulips and various annuals each year.

'IT CAPTURES MY HEART BECAUSE IT'S EVER-CHANGING, EVERY YEAR IT'S DIFFERENT.'

Butter grew up on a farm in Baltimore, USA, into a family of gardeners; her maternal grandparents had a beautiful garden outside Philadelphia, while her mother was a president of the local Garden Club of America. She moved to New York to work at Christie's, before emigrating to London in 1988, with her then husband, and working as an assistant at Colefax & Fowler in the era of many design greats, including Imogen Taylor, Tom Parr, Roger Banks-Pye and Chester Jones. Both roles gave her a love of design and an understanding of composition, form and colour. After having children, and realising that being in the garden was what made her most happy, Butter took some short courses at The English Gardening School and then a year-long diploma in Plants & Plantsmanship, before taking on her first design commission for a friend in nearby Hammersmith.

She moved to her Victorian villa in Stamford Brook in 1992. And the style of the garden she has created here echoes her professional work which spans smart townhouse gardens in London and Bath, including schemes for interior designers Rita Konig and Matilda Goad, as well as larger country projects. The meadow of her own garden has been such a hit that it's a frequent request from clients and most of her gardens include some topiarised forms.

'I have to have a clipped shape,' says Butter, whose own borders are grounded with a series of yew pyramids. 'What I really like is chaos and lots of rich, multi-layered planting, but it only works if there is a strong framework of shrubs and clipped shapes to bring order to the abundant tangle. The topiary almost disappears in the summer, but in the wintertime it really holds the garden together.' That love of form is also played out in clipped evergreens and trees in pots too; her back door is framed by standards of *Myrtus communis* pruned into neat balls and multistem *Osmanthus x burkwoodii*.

Her early experience working in interior design has also been key to her practice, channelling the interior style of homes through to the garden. She also believes that the client's relationship with their garden designer can be just as intimate, too: 'With exteriors, we are always editing, revisiting regularly and having further discussions – it's a growing space.'

For Butter, her own garden is a therapeutic space, forcing her to slow down. It marks the beginning of the weekend. 'I come out here on Friday evening and cut flowers for the house and really feel set up and ready for the weekend. I would be lost without it.'

MARY KEEN

GLOUCESTERSHIRE

Viewed from the high street of pretty stone façades, there's little hint of the bucolic scene that lies beyond the front door of Mary Keen's Gloucestershire home. But step through the kitchen doors into the garden that she has created over the past seven years and there are pretty courtyards, borders of much-loved plants and a meandering path through a meadow peppered with a succession of treasured bulbs and wildflowers. 'It's lovely that in this little town you can have a garden where it feels like you can get lost', says the prolific designer and writer.

Mary moved here with her late husband, Charles, in 2017 from The Old Rectory, a handsome Georgian house in the Cotswolds where they had created a two-acre garden set amidst many more acres of woodland and pasture. When they arrived at their new home there was lawn, an unappealing terrace and a boundary of *Cupressus* hedging. She opened up the space by removing the dense hedging, which in turn liberated a magnolia – one of a handful of trees she kept, including a silver leaf pear, an old apple and a winter-flowering cherry.

Downsizing to a garden 'the size of two tennis courts' focusses the mind. The kitchen leads directly out to a sunny, sheltered courtyard filled with pots that begin with colourful spring bulbs followed by a collection of pelargoniums including 'Copthorne'. Also enjoying the sheltered conditions here are *Fuchsia* 'Lady Boothby', *Plumbago capensis* and *Coronilla glauca 'Citrina'* while the lush fern, *Polystichum setiferum* 'Bevis', can be admired at close quarters.

Mary had the existing York stone taken up here, replacing it with lighter Cotswold hoggin to brighten up the space and allow a few self-seeders such as the dusky rose and lemon *Linaria* 'Peachy' or *Geranium pyrenaicum* 'Bill Wallis' to grow in the gravel. On the walls there are climbers including *Rosa* x *odorata* 'Mutabilis', *R.* 'Bengal Crimson' and the double white form of *R. banksiae*.

A path with rose arches runs along the side of a garden studio, leading to a shadier courtyard where there are favourite spring plants including *Daphne bholua* 'Jacqueline Postill', sweet wood anemones (*Anemone* x *lipsiensis),* primulas and vinca, as well as euphorbia.

Everything in Mary's garden is about close observation, the day-to-day process of gardening. And it's completely different to those created for her clients, who unsurprisingly are unlikely to be doing the gardening. 'But that is what interests me and that's what I love', she explains. 'It's about everyday watchfulness and the kind of tiny changes that you make if you're a gardener. You go out and if you see something is not quite right, you change it slightly.' Here there are many places in the garden to sit and observe: 'I like gardens where I think "I'd like to stay here" rather than "Wow, that's amazing."'

It's about careful selection too, seeking out the very best forms of plants such as the rich, darker Great Dixter form of *Gladiolus byzantinus* that flowers in the meadow, or the *Malus hupehensis* Mary has planted here – another Dixter purchase. Although not horticulturally trained, her immense knowledge has accrued over a lifetime of looking (she sat on the National Trust gardens panel for three decades) and continual dialogue with gardening friends, such as the plantsman Jonny Bruce, designer Pip Morrison who she worked with for many years, or Isabel and Julian Bannerman

'I LIKE GARDENS WHERE I THINK "I'D LIKE TO STAY HERE" RATHER THAN "WOW, THAT'S AMAZING."'

who first recommended moving to the pretty Gloucestershire village. 'I love other gardeners', Mary says. 'I love the exchange. How's this doing? Could this be better? What form have you got? *Everyone* has always got a better form.'

That community spirit is very much in evidence in the meadow where friends have contributed orchids, bladder campion and cowslips (a few days after we meet another friend sends the most precious of parcels – three carefully packaged bee orchids). Arguably the garden's main focus is this transporting area, cut through with a curving path that leads to a charming stone playhouse, added by a previous owner. Mary began here by allowing the existing lawn to grow and added yellow rattle and a succession of bulbs including snowdrops, crocuses and narcissi (the delicate Jonquils are favoured as they die back more elegantly in the grass). There's *Anemone blanda* and *A. pavonina* and wildflowers including geraniums and scabious. Each season the scene changes; one year wild carrot dominates in summer, the following year it's a sea of daisies.

Mary has added a small orchard of favourite apples too – 'Ashmead's Kernel', 'Discovery' and 'Egremont Russet' – but conscious of time passing, she invested in mature apple trees ('I thought I am so old I can't wait'), knowing full well that she would always tell clients to buy small trees. Clambering over an arbour behind them is a 'Francis E. Lester' rose, which has single flowers similar to apple blossom, followed by dense sprays of red hips.

There are roses dotted throughout the garden – 'Paul's Himalayan Musk' scrambles up beside the playhouse, 'Albertine' climbs over one of the lovely stone walls that form the boundary. But many of the roses bear simple single flowers that work with the naturalistic effect of the meadow, such as the intense red *Rosa* 'Scharlachglut', *R. moyesii* and *R. hugonis*.

Moving from a sizeable garden to a smaller town garden has been liberating for Mary, even if at first her children could not see how she would make sense of it. 'The big garden had got quite demanding. I was always rushing around, or waiting for another coach to arrive. And this is lovely, because I can just garden and fiddle with it and it doesn't really matter.' There are brilliant space-saving ideas too; the clever walk-through greenhouse was an idea plucked from Parham House and Burford Priory, where she made a garden for Matthew Freud and Elisabeth Murdoch. The garden also spills out into a secret village passage where the planting continues right out past her close neighbours. In addition, Mary grows vegetables on a nearby allotment.

Mary began making gardens in her twenties, encouraged in part by her mother-in-law who was a painter and gardener. Charles was a banker and they often moved house, so she was 'always making a new garden'. Her friends then asked her to design their gardens too. One day at Newbury races, she sat next to Charles Wintour, who was then editor of the *Evening Standard*, and he asked if she would be interested in writing the paper's gardening column. She worked as their gardening columnist for eight years before moving on to *The Independent* and then *The Daily Telegraph*, always writing in tandem with her design work.

She has made gardens for the late Lord Rothschild (including Eythrope which was the subject of her 2015 book *Paradise and Plenty: A Rothschild Family Garden)* and she designed the gardens around the opera house at Glyndebourne. Her current projects – or rather those she's able to talk about – include the gardens of George and Amal Clooney's homes in the UK and the south of France.

Mary has no desire to stop designing – or writing. She's currently working on a new book, on the day-by-day experience of making a garden. For her, gardens are not something to simply look at, they are 'places to be'. 'I want to get lost in it', she adds looking out over the meadow. 'It's a wonderful area to work in. It's a lovely thing to spend time thinking about plants and flowers.'

CATHERINE FITZGERALD

WILTSHIRE

After negotiating the narrow, twisting lanes of north Wiltshire, it's immediately apparent when Catherine FitzGerald's home looms into view. It's not the big oak barrel, denoting the 18th-century property's former life as a brewery, but the mad froth of flowers that spills forth from the house that gives it away. Roses including 'New Dawn', 'Albrighton Rambler' and 'The Garland' clamber up to the mullion windows, or fall over the stone wall that marks the boundary. There's clipped yew topiary, nurtured from feathered whips, and hundreds of ox-eye daisies, foxgloves and a scattering of buttercups.

A beautiful honeysuckle, *Lonicera etrusca* 'Michael Rosse', shrouds a north-facing wall, underplanted with *Dryopteris filix mas*. It's all soft, loose and romantic. 'The little front garden spoke to me. I wanted it to look like it had always been there, in harmony with the lichen covered stone roof tiles and mottled lime mortar of the walls,' explains Catherine, who arrived at the house in 2018 with her husband, the actor Dominic West, and their four children. 'I really believe in working with the spirit of the place, responding to the building, to the landscape.'

Brewing stopped here in the 1930s but its imprint remains in the louvre windows, a huge industrial water tank and a huge chimney that rises comically through the rear of the building. As they renovated, they moved from the darker front of the house to the sunny south-west-facing brewery side. And just as the house has distinct elements, so too does the garden.

She started by making a south-facing terrace, where the reclaimed York stone paving and gravel erupts with *Alchemilla mollis*, Mexican daisies, lavender, fennel and evening primrose seeding through the cracks. Large pots of lush bananas and magenta salvias bask in the sunshine with *Phlomis* bordering the kitchen door. Next came the central courtyard, with a series of beds in the stony, post-industrial ground. The peeling cast iron water tank for the old brewery was filled with rain water from a downpipe – it now has two little bubbling water spouts.

'I'm really interested in scale and contrast,' says the designer. 'Tiny things and giant things.' There are towering cardoons and the statuesque grey Scotch thistle *Onopordum acanthium*: 'I am obsessed with them – they tend to seed and I dig them up and put them in places.'

There are shrub roses such as 'Wilhelm' ('a brilliant rose that repeats all summer') and sumptuous Bourbon roses including 'Comte de Chambord' and 'Jacques Cartier'. Two *Rosa* x *odorata* 'Mutabilis' are climbing up the front of the house, planted into enormous pots that Dominic discovered on a walking trip in Cornwall. The colour is cut through with the intense lime green of *Euphorbia wallichii* and *E. seguieriana* subsp. *niciciana*. There are self-seeders galore – orange poppies, wild strawberries, foxgloves, *Macleaya cordata* and *Knautia macedonica*.

This garden is nothing like Catherine's family home at Glin Castle, on the Shannon Estuary in the west of Ireland, where the temperate climate is moderated by the Gulf Stream and subtropical and exotic species flourish. Her childhood there with her late father Desmond, the 29th Knight of Glin, and her mother Olda Willes, who restored the walled garden, and her younger sisters made her 'very keyed into atmosphere' long before she thought about a career around plants.

There were lots of childhood garden visits, too; she recalls one visit to Derreen Garden in County Kerry, where she was confronted with a Jurassic wilderness of tree ferns, self-seeded rhododendrons, mosses, lichen and huge rocks: 'It was so exciting. I remember the hairs standing up on the back of my neck.' She studied English and History of Art at Trinity College Dublin and thought she would become a writer. It took many more years before she realised plants were her passion.

She trained as a horticultural apprentice with the Royal Horticultural Society at Wisley for two years, and went to work for Arabella Lennox-Boyd as a planting designer, where she worked across many projects and visited Arabella's favourite

'I REALLY BELIEVE IN WORKING WITH THE SPIRIT OF THE PLACE, RESPONDING TO THE BUILDING, TO THE LANDSCAPE.'

gardens including Ninfa in Italy. 'At that point I thought "ok, this is it"', says Catherine. 'Working on gardens, with plants and meeting garden people gave me a whole life I hadn't had, and it gave me a purpose. It's such an encompassing life.'

Her big solo break came working on Glenarm Castle where she helped with a redesign of the walled garden, installing a hugely successful mount. With a young family and growing commissions, she started to collaborate with landscape architect Mark Lutyens, forming an enduring partnership, Lutyens & FitzGerald Landscape Design. They were commissioned to work on the restoration of the walled garden at Hillsborough Castle, a project spanning six years. Alongside this, Catherine regularly returns to Glin Castle, which she has run as an exclusive hire property since 2017, and where she continues to develop the landscape, including a woodland garden with tree ferns, an exotic bog garden and wildflower meadow, adding to the planting of previous generations.

The garden in Wiltshire gives her the opportunity to play with an entirely different palette of plants, growing things that would not survive the damp Irish climate. 'Here it's brash and limey and quite cold,' she explains. But it's also more experimental too. 'I didn't stick to the garden masterplan – it evolved. I've made so many mistakes with it, but I've learnt so much.'

The pastoral setting is bolstered by sheep that roam the surrounding fields and two Oxford Sandy and Black pigs. And to the rear of the house Dominic has built a swimming pond, teaching himself by watching videos by organic pool pioneer David Pagan Butler, who has since mentored his fledgling pond. Around the margins there are waterlilies, mint, bullrushes, flag iris and purple loosestrife: 'In the evening, all the swallows come and swoop into the water. There are damselflies and dragonflies and it's absolutely a revelation.'

To the west, she removed the existing amoeba-shaped beds and has developed meadows and an orchard, adding *Rosa* 'Complicata' ('it only flowers for a few weeks but it's so wild and luscious'), lilacs, *Philadelphus* and clipped yew to the garden's existing fruit trees, which include a beautiful, sculptural old apple tree. It has taken about six years for yellow rattle to take hold here and suppress the grass so that wildflowers can flourish. 'I love a garden to feel natural, loose, relaxed – as if it's just doing its thing,' adds Catherine. 'But that requires careful orchestration – I am usually paddling frantically under the surface to keep up the illusion – I think Dominic thinks it has just happened all on its own!'

Her latest project is the Festival of Gardens and Nature, which held its inaugral event at Ballintubbert Gardens in County Laois in 2024 with a weekend of talks on plants, gardens, ecology and environment, and one day she hopes that it can be held at Glin Castle. 'We are always on the go here and there,' Catherine says of their peripatetic family life. 'As the children get bigger, I think I won't have to rush back and forth so much.' Her heart is clearly very much in Ireland, but for now at least she's at home in her thriving Wiltshire garden.

ISABEL AND JULIAN BANNERMAN

SOMERSET

In the introduction to their 2016 monograph, *Landscape of Dreams*, Isabel and Julian Bannerman detail their endless quest to discover their next project: 'We dream, waking and sleeping, about architecture and landscape, derelict houses and shattered gardens, imagined and actual.... This curious searching brought us together.'

The serial doer-uppers have spent a lifetime in this all-consuming hunt. Renovating and making on an epic scale, first at the abandoned baroque house, The Ivy in Chippenham, Wiltshire, then at dreamy Hanham Court, near Bristol, where they moved in 1993 and spent almost two decades. They moved again in 2012, to Trematon, the motte-and-bailey castle owned by the Duchy of Cornwall.

Their current project is Ashington Manor, a beguiling Elizabethan house close to the River Yeo in south Somerset and adjoining the 13th-century St Vincent's church. The house was reduced by half by a fire in the early 19th century, and had been empty for 10 years when they found it. It was not, however, love at first sight.

'I pushed for coming here more than Julian,' says Isabel, sitting in their glorious Gothick kitchen. She had always wanted to live in a hamstone house. 'We didn't think we were going to end up here, I can tell you,' adds Julian, who was more preoccupied with the flat and relatively characterless land. 'There isn't even a bank to put a primrose. So it had to have the structure in the beginning. And I wasn't going to wait 40 years.'

They ringfenced a pot of money and invested in mature topiary, installing an avenue of enormous yew beehive topiaries stretching from north to south, forming an uncompromising central axis across the garden. 'We got them before we even started the building work,' says Isabel. 'And we didn't lose any.'

When they arrived there wasn't much garden to speak of – one Irish yew, an avenue of *Catalpa* lining the drive and lawn that had been fastidiously cut for decades. They let the grass grow long around the drive and then planted rambling roses and lilacs, including *Syringa* 'Prince Wolkonsky', 'Beauty of Moscow', 'Souvenir de Louis Spaeth' and 'Firmament' – a 'thundery' grey-violet. Meanwhile, in the grass five orchids emerged (now in their hundreds), which they then supplemented with thousands more earlier-flowering bulbs, including narcissi Actaea', the later flowering *N. poeticus* var. *recurvus* and fritillaries, which are all followed by white camassias and white Martagon lilies.

A shrubbery had been long planted close to the house, and beyond it an orchard. To join the two areas, Julian began to plant a spring garden under the shade of a nut tree. Here *Euphorbia characias* subsp. *wulfenii* is surrounded by ferns, *Daphne odora* and a succession of spring flowers, including snowdrops, aconites, single hellebores, hardy geraniums and astrantia. Later, there are Martagon lilies and young *Cardiocrinum giganteum* plants. The mature plants of the giant Himalayan lily, which can take seven years to flower and can reach 4 metres (13 feet), are already flowering close by, with their big trumpet lily flowers and amazing seedheads.

The couple met in Edinburgh, where Isabel studied history. In the second term of her first year she met Julian, who ran his eponymous bar, Bannermans. They married one year

‘IT’S BROAD-BRUSHSTROKES COLOUR AND STRUCTURE. IT’S JUST ABOUT GREAT THINGS WE LIKE.’

later. Their shared passion for country houses, antiques and gardens was passed down from their parents. Julian had grown up immersed in gardens by his mother and studied fine art at Oxford’s Ruskin School of Art before later working in contemporary art and the Edinburgh festival. As a girl, Isabel was pouring through *Country Life* and receiving a grounding in art and design history from her antiques-dealer mother.

In 1991 they set up I & J Bannerman. Their first commission was for the writer and journalist Candida Lycett Green who in turn introduced them to the then Prince of Wales. They started by doing ‘tiny, tiny’ things at Highgrove but went on to create the Temple Grove, perhaps better known as the Stumpery. Their work on both the gardens and architectural renovation of the Dairy at Lord Rothchild’s Waddesdon Manor in Buckinghamshire, which went on to win the 1992 Europa Nostra Heritage Award, became a springboard for other projects. They became known for their follies and theatrical flourishes, and worked on a string of notable projects at Houghton Hall, Arundel Castle, Euridge Manor Farm and Wychwood Manor.

Those grand country house projects are known for their exuberant planting with roses clambering over mellow brick walls, rambling through trees and in fountains across meadows, as they do at another well-known project, Asthall Manor in Oxfordshire. At Ashington they’ve planted endless ramblers and climbers as well as a rose garden enclosed by yew hedging. ‘I call it the conventional garden…because it’s so obvious,’ says Isabel. Here old varieties including ‘Tuscany Superb’ flourish alongside clumps of mostly white perennials including peonies, *Crambe cordifolia*, *Phlox paniculata* ‘David’, *Thalictrum* ‘Splendide White’ and the cheerful white daisies of *Leucanthemum* x *superbum*. ‘We hadn’t had many roses in Cornwall so we wanted to get back to them,’ she adds. ‘Rambling roses are so much easier than anything else, you can’t go wrong.’

Varieties including ‘Perennial Blue’ and ‘The Garland’ cover the south-facing stone wall on the far side of the garden, and opposite on the cool north-facing wall of the house they’ve planted ‘Madame Alfred Carrière’ which has covered serious ground in just a few years. Isabel puts their health down to the good alluvial soil here, as well as her husband’s plant whispering: ‘Julian has tied them in and talked to them and they are very vigorous.’

Beyond the rose garden, beds of *Lavandula angustifolia* stretch out from the house. Alongside are shrub roses, nicotiana and hazel wigwams with homegrown sweet peas, flanking a croquet lawn, and punctuated by big bushy clumps of *Salvia rosmarinus*, which all chimes with the Elizabethan architecture of the house.

Further across, a double border pours forth from Isabel’s studio, where the couple lived when they were restoring the main house and now also the site of a cottage to rent. A riotous collection of perennials in kaleidoscopic colour fills two long beds that stretch down to a secluded seating area enveloped by wisteria-covered walls.

Joyful lupins, delphiniums, foxgloves, hollyhocks, roses, geums, nigella and poppies are edged with more lavender, tiny dianthus, *Erigeron karvinskianus* and bearded iris. ‘We don’t agonise about whether it’s this cultivar or that cultivar,’ explains Isabel. ‘It’s broad brushstrokes colour and structure. It’s just about great things we like.’ And their approach in their own garden is far more experimental than in their clients’ gardens where they cannot risk putting some tiny interesting plant that may or may not work.

In the middle of the wall, an opening flanked by one of the couple’s signature oak posts topped with ball finials leads into another lawn, where an old scout tent with scarlet poles stands through summer. Here there are new borders of bearded iris made from divisions of their collection – the only plants they brought with them when they bought the house.

All around are pots filled with vivid lilies – although Isabel’s collection of containers (almost always large pots, which mean less watering) is also scattered throughout a rear courtyard at the back of the house.

Both are hands-on, practical gardeners, although there are, of course, never enough hours in the day to maintain it all. Julian’s preference is for builders or labourers over gardeners: ‘He doesn’t want skilled help in the garden – he doesn’t want anyone with ideas or opinions,’ explains Isabel. ‘Including me!’

And yet despite being so hands-on in their own gardens, they are sanguine when they move on. ‘I don’t think it affects us very much – it’s funny,’ says Isabel of the gardens that they have left behind. ‘It sounds terribly disloyal,’ adds Julian. But creating places is what drives them on and it is, says Isabel, a potent and exciting pursuit. They’ve already toyed with moving on from Ashington after hearing from someone who was interested in buying their house. ‘Water is something I would have loved,’ muses Julian, recalling a recent discovery in Ross-on-Wye. ‘Water brings a whole other dimension,’ adds Isabel. And with that they are off, plotting and planning and thinking of more landscapes of dreams.

LIBBY RUSSELL

SOMERSET

When Libby Russell first came to Somerset to view Batcombe House in the summer of 2001, the vendor dropped off the landscape architect and her husband, Alexander Russell, in the meadows that sweep across the valley opposite the house. Snaking around the River Alham, the landscape has views to the Bronze Age fort, Small Down Knoll and, in the distance, to Glastonbury Tor. The ancient land here is sculpted by striations made from centuries of sheep grazing and is rich with wildflowers that hum with bees and butterflies.

By the time Libby reached the handsome 18th-century rectory, the challenge of an awkwardly sloping and damp blank canvas of 3 acres didn't faze her. Like all homeseekers who have lost their minds over a dreamy plot, she knew she could figure it out.

The garden Libby has created over the past two decades splits those three acres into two areas. On one side, a series of terraced gardens, each distinctly different in mood and planting, is all about the demands of family life, with a productive kitchen garden, greenhouses, swimming pool and cleverly concealed tennis court. On the other side of the plot, divided by a wall built in local stone and a huge listed cedar, is a cooler, more contemplative space where sweeping borders and a grassed amphitheatre are all designed on curves.

Top of her wishlist was a kitchen where she could see straight out into the garden, and the first in a series of terraces does exactly this. A central lawn is bordered by a herb garden and frothing borders that are a riot of exuberant colour – mounds of *Rosa gallica* 'Versicolor' or the soft pink *R.* 'Felicia', *Nepeta* 'Six Hills Giant', penstemon, phlox, hardy geraniums and poppies, which are all followed later in the season by hundreds of salvias and dahlias.

This intensively cultivated area is full of hard-working plants that are both long flowering and well behaved (Libby is a long-standing member of the RHS Herbaceous Plant Committee), such as the vivid magenta *Geranium* 'Dragon Heart' ('a good geranium that's on steroids this year'). Every available wall here is covered in roses, including 'Madame Caroline Testout', 'American Pillar' and 'De Rescht'. The garden is primarily about the herbaceous planting in pinks and purples, but a border with ten yew pyramids introduces a more pointillist mood, with dots of colour creating the overall picture; there's *Phlomoides tuberosa* 'Amazone' and *Eryngium* x *zabelii* 'Big Blue' along with more phlox, salvias, astrantias, foxgloves and larkspurs.

There's structure here, too – a line of espalier *Malus toringo* encloses the north side of the garden and two clipped *Pyrus salicifolia* 'Pendula' punctuate a rectangular pond where Libby rehomed some native crayfish that were discovered on the site. 'I've learnt that structure from topiary and evergreens is important to anchor the winter view,' explains Libby, who actively gardens for winter seedheads. 'If you can get it to have its moment in winter as well as the summer, it's a joy.'

Up some steps, the mood shifts in the equally exuberant and multi-layered ornamental kitchen garden with hoggin paths, woven hazel gates and fruit trees trained as espaliers, cordons and goblets. Designed on a south-east facing slope visible from the house, this productive space takes its cue from the French

'I'VE LEARNT THAT STRUCTURE FROM TOPIARY AND EVERGREENS IS IMPORTANT TO ANCHOR THE WINTER VIEW.'

potager style, with lettuce, beetroot, chard, spinach and annuals for cutting, all arranged in contrasting lines and blocks. Here you will find sweet peas on hazel wigwams, gourds and beans hanging from hazel tunnels and perennial beds of asparagus, rhubarb and shrub roses. 'If you're going to grow chard why not grow it in a pretty row', Libby says, pointing out the backlit leaves, which to her are just as beautiful as the line of nearby *Papaver* 'Amazing Grey'. 'There's no reason in a vegetable garden why you can't have that succesion of fruit and flowers.'

Up on the next levels, where a pool and pool house sit below a tennis court, the look becomes deliberately untamed, with fuzzy banks of wildflowers mixed in with huge fountains of species roses. There are more trained apple trees for screening, buddleias to provide colour when the roses go over and a succession of Martagon lilies, scabious and valerian all flowering in the long grass. Here, the pastoral borders link with the surrounding meadows, because, she says, 'It's all about views across the valley.'

Libby grew up with beautiful landscapes. As the niece of the Duke of Rutland, her childhood homes included the 16,000-acre Belvoir Castle estate in Leicestershire and Haddon Hall in Derbyshire. After completing her postgraduate degree in Landscape Architecture at the University of Greenwich, she worked for Arabella Lennox-Boyd before founding her own studio, Mazzullo + Russell, with Emma Mazzullo in 2014.

In her own garden Libby has the space for experimentation, and nowhere is that more apparent that in the sweeping border and sculpted landforms that slope up from the rear of the house. Here, the palette is soft and soothing with mounds of cloud-pruned box and tiered lawns leading the eye to her border of big plants; clipped yews, *Sarcococca* and *Sesleria* provide a contrast to flowering shrubs, which include deutzia, magnolia and cornus and big perennials such as *Nepeta* 'Romany Dusk', followed by a succession of hydrangeas and hard-working roses such as 'Sally Holmes', a long-flowering floribunda with blush white flowers. 'It's all planted in a rhythmic way and nothing up here is small', explains Libby. The maintenance here is a fraction of the continually refreshed borders closer to the house: 'Up here it's more a case of taking things out to keep the balance. Plants are like children, you've got to keep them in order the whole time, and everybody has to have their own space.'

A long, shaded border of thriving supersize perennials surrounds a sweet grotto and leads back down to the house, where the mood shifts again. Close to the house, where Libby wants to be able to sit and enjoy the garden, the palette is calm with white, and greens with subtle hints of colour from a pale blue clematis or 'Buff Beauty' roses. Climbing roses scramble up the north-facing walls, while clipped box balls punctuate a door into the house. Here the focus is cleverly directed to a rectangular bed, four metres (13 feet) long by two metres (six feet) wide, filled with airy white daisies. Like everywhere else in the garden, this patch is orchestrated for a year-round view, starting with snowdrops in late winter, then black and white fritillaries, white alliums and summer wildflowers, including *Succisa pratensis,* which will bring structure until the end of the year. 'This is no-gardening gardening,' she says. 'And I think it's my favourite bed in the whole garden. You don't have to have a big area to have something that's special.'

EMILY ERLAM

LONDON

Looking out from the expansive glass walls of Emily Erlam's serene and cool basement kitchen, it's easy to forget that we are right in the centre of the city, and just a stone's throw from the relentless London traffic thundering along the Euston Road. From floor to ceiling there are lush, green leaves; huge fans of *Fatsia japonica* spread out against a backdrop of neatly clipped *Choisya* x *dewitteana* 'Aztec Pearl', valued here for its glossy plump foliage, rather than its scented white flowers.

There are mounds of *Pittosporum tenuifolium* 'Golf Ball', the velvety pale green, felted leaves of *Ballota pseudodictamnus* and, close to the boundary, the unusual *Stachyurus praecox* – a deciduous Japanese native with strands of creamy yellow flowers in late winter. On the wall next to it, the cinnamon-barked myrtle *Luma apiculata* is informally cloud pruned. Amidst the greenery there's an occasional flash of colour – the pink-tinged blooms of *Rosa* 'Pierre de Ronsard' trained on the wall, or the delicate flowers of *Fuchsia magellanica* var. *molinae* that hang over a Belgian stone-topped dining table.

'I'm very focused on feeling,' says the designer on a garden's ability to spark an emotional response. 'And with plants we can create a sense of drama quite quickly.' Here, those effects are dialled up to the max with layers of evergreen shrubs, elegant trees and breezy perennials and grasses creating an immersive jungle.

When Emily arrived here, she was faced with the typical terraced-house plot – a long, narrow runway with a characterless path running its length. The garden is also north-facing, so she used the spoil from building work to create a sequence of four terraces through the garden. 'As you rise up, you get sun at different times of the day', explains the designer. 'But it also gives you a sense of journey.'

While there was an existing brick wall at the end of the garden, she had the other boundary walls rebuilt in London stock bricks. Paths were made in stone setts with the treatment for each terrace responding to the planting – on the dining terrace there are limestone flags, creating a seamless flow from the kitchen inside to the outside space. The second terrace, shaded by a crabapple tree and styled as a lounge area with elegant furniture, has pale gravel bouncing light into the shaded areas, with soothing evergreen planting including *Trachelospermum jasminoides* and clipped *Ilex crenata, Buxus sempervirens* and more *Pittosporum* in terracotta pots sourced from Hode Pottery in Kent.

On the sunny top terrace, which has a wilder, more relaxed feeling, she has experimented with a Japanese paving technique, combining huge stone slabs, known as scarps, that are shaved off as the top layer in quarries. 'It's like the crust of the bread. You can buy them cheaply and there's a really organic shape to it. I just really love large-format stuff.' Around the huge textural slabs, smaller pieces in the same stone are skilfully slotted in.

Circling a central fire pit there are plants that are prized for their interesting form, including banks of *Echium pininana*, the giant *Tetrapanax papyrifer* 'Rex', toothed-leaved *Melianthus major* and an *Albizia*, the Persian silk tree, providing distinctive fern-like foliage as well as fluffy pink flowers in high summer. *Buddleja davidii* 'Black Knight' has been fan-trained across the tall boundary brick wall, alongside the climbing rose 'Cécile Brünner', with its luscious pale pink flowers.

'I'M VERY FOCUSED ON FEELING... WITH PLANTS WE CAN CREATE A SENSE OF DRAMA QUITE QUICKLY.'

Trees throughout the garden have been chosen not just for their beautiful shapes and foliage but also for a succession of flowers. After the early flowering *Stachyurus praecox,* the crab apple flowers in the centre of the garden are followed by the creamy bracts of a *Cornus kousa* var. *chinensis* further up the space. Despite the cohesive feeling here, Emily insists that the planting has come together organically over time. 'This isn't really a designed garden,' she explains. 'This is an osmosis of things that have been left over from other projects. And it's quite liberating.'

Emily originally worked as a researcher at the BBC, first on arts documentaries, including Alan Yentob's *Imagine* series, before working on *Newsnight Review*. Pregnant with her first child, and having taken a short course at The English Gardening School, she just became 'really switched onto' plants. She had to wait two years before retraining at the London College of Garden Design, but filled that time with reading and visiting gardens and immersing herself in the subject. By the time she got to college, she was ready to hit the ground running. 'I was so thirsty for it,' she recalls.

Her first project when she left college was a gravel garden for an architect and designer in Dungeness, who she'd met through her husband. In lieu of payment she had a two-week holiday at the house, and the time allowed her to tap into the spirit of the landscape. From the top of the lighthouse tower she mapped out the landforms that had been created by wind erosion in the local landscape and planned the garden using the same shapes. Densely planted rosemary, sea kale, sedums, santolina and drought-tolerant herbs and shrubs were then planted tightly around a converted industrial building. Dotted throughout were decorative arrangements of stones and fragments from the building's past. 'It was a small but really challenging space. It felt to me like an installation', says Emily. 'I think there's an element of designing gardens that you don't have to have training for. It's a bit like being an artist. You have to be able to channel a vision.'

Her own garden has a cooly contemporary feel. In her studio, she works alongside architects (one of the most beautiful borrowed aspects of her own garden is a neighbouring Victorian factory building, recently converted by the architect Thomas Heatherwick) and there's a very defined instinct for materiality and architecture in her work. But underlying this is a deep interest in form. 'I've always been interested right from the beginning in mounds and fountains,' she says of her predilection for neatly clipped shapes in all sizes planted underneath arching shrubs and trees that flow throughout the garden.

An appreciation of foliage is ever-present here, too; on the second terrace *Cercis canadensis* 'Forest Pansy' and *Rosa* x *odorata* 'Mutabilis' sit alongside a favourite *Edgeworthia chrysantha* with lush, decorative leaves. Steps away, geraniums and *Melica altissima* 'Alba' are contrasted with another favoured plant – *Bergenia*, an unusual and perhaps unfashionable choice but a winning one. 'I feel like maybe part of making a garden is to set your ego aside', adds Emily. 'Just focus on what the space is telling you and make it happen.'

ALASDAIR CAMERON

DEVON

It's the dying days of summer at Silver Street Farm in Devon and all hands are on deck. Landscape designer Alasdair Cameron is sizing up a seasonal sharpening of his hedges and topiary; his sons, Oscar and Kit, are hard at work taming the meadow boundaries, and his daughter, Jemima, is cutting stems for a floral display in the kitchen. It's just as well that there's a collaborative spirit here because this is not a garden for the faint-hearted.

When Alasdair and his wife, Tor, discovered the property in 2011 it was a working dairy farm. The only garden was a small area to the front of the 17th-century farmhouse enclosed by listed wrought-iron railings, and most of the 3 acres of land around the house and expansive barns was given over to grazing.

Alasdair began reimagining the land at the rear by opening up rural views to the east and to the west, where an overgrown stream snaked through the property. The surrounding tree outlines were then echoed within the garden through many hawthorn, hazel and field maple trees, and in topiary forms in beech, hornbeam and yew. But the grandest gesture here is the epic long border which stretches 60 metres (200 feet) from one end of the garden to the other, starting narrow and gradually widening into a triangle, with curving paths cut like rivulets into the planting. Tightly clipped low yew domes add punctuation points, sometimes sitting outside the border's edge and sometimes immersed in a froth of planting.

Waves of colour and texture flow through the border with an emphasis on big-impact plants, including *Eupatorium maculatum, Miscanthus* x *giganteus, Phlox paniculata, Salvia involucrata* 'Hadspen', *Persicaria* and the towering *Eryngium pandanifolium*. There are asters, veronicastrums, *Baptisia australis* and feathery grasses dotted throughout. Self-seeded fennel, *Knautia* and *Succisa pratensis* make an appearance too, and along the front of the border *Calamintha nepeta, Pennisetum,* verbenas and a collection of *Origanum*, chosen for its excellent form in winter, add another layer of colour and texture.

Piet Oudolf is a strong influence here – winter trips to the Dutch designer's eponymous field at Hauser & Wirth's Bruton outpost have informed the planting; a case in point is the enormous purple-flowered *Vernonia arkansana* now emerging in the border.

Even if there's a succession of colour, the border is designed with winter seedheads in mind. When the family arrived here, there was little birdlife, but more than a decade on and the birds are now abundant, feeding on the copious berries and seedheads throughout the colder months. Alasdair cuts the whole border back in February, leaving all waste in situ to rot down into the soil so that nothing is taken away. As fresh growth emerges, there are alliums for early spring colour. Self-seeders are celebrated, so that each year the balance shifts with a sudden surge of *Digitalis* or a sea of poppies. 'I'm constantly playing,' says Alasdair. 'I wanted a large canvas to paint on. Every year it kept getting bigger, it became a standing joke.'

He's had a weakness for magnificent borders since visiting gardens in his late teens, learning from Nori and Sandra Pope's planting at Hadspen, or the planting at Barnsley House and Great Dixter. 'With a shorter border you are limited with how much flow you can get, and you can't move through lots of different planting experiences.'

'I'M CONSTANTLY PLAYING… I WANTED A LARGE CANVAS TO PAINT ON. EVERY YEAR IT KEPT GETTING BIGGER.'

Alasdair left school a year early and went to study interior design and history of art in Kent. He became fascinated by great landscape designers of the 18th century, such as Capability Brown and Humphry Repton, and began visiting gardens and nurseries, and collecting plants – a lifelong habit that meant when he arrived at Silver Street Farm he had abundant plant stock.

His next stop was Merrist Wood College, where studying landscape architecture included learning 50 plants each week. He still remembers his first: *Caryopteris* × *clandonensis* 'Kew Blue'. 'Having failed at school it was an extraordinary experience to be good at something,' he says. In his early 20s Alasdair worked for garden designer Helen Dorrien-Smith ('an extraordinary plantswoman who taught me beyond measure') and when she retired a couple of years later he took on her clients and also went on to build several gardens for Arabella Lennox-Boyd, forming his own eponymous firm in 1992. As well as taking on design projects, his large London-based team also builds and maintains gardens.

In many ways his own garden is a place to unleash his creativity, playing with new plants, combinations and ideas. Since moving here he's become much more interested in ornamental grasses, which significantly contribute to the garden's atmosphere. In contrast to the long border, a bank of grasses creates a stepping stone into the fields beyond. There's a huge swathe of *Molinia* 'Heidebraut', providing autumn colour and winter structure, interplanted here with *Achillea* and *Allium sphaerocephalon*. Alongside it all are blocks of *Calamagrostis* and a lush, sculpted mound of chamomile lawn, added as a contrast to the diaphanous grasses.

Running parallel to the long border, a more restrained stretch of planting, including huge clumps of *Persicaria* and *Rudbeckia*, echoes the warm tones of the rusty tin roof and red stone walls of the huge barn that stands behind it. The numerous expansive exterior walls provide seemingly endless opportunity for climbers here. By the barn there's a sunken garden and a 'paved meadow', where self-seeders including *Deschampsia*, *Achillea*, thyme and marjoram are gradually taking over a terrace.

At the front of the house the height and drama of the long border is realised on a smaller scale. There's silvery *Onopordum*, *Eupatorium*, *Deschampsia*, *Eryngium yuccifolium* and self-sown teasels, while *Verbascum olympicum* echoes the lemon-painted façade of the house. A single multistem hornbeam adds a strong counterpoint to the hazy mass of plants.

Roses, including 'Mutabilis', 'Lady Hillingdon', 'Chevy Chase' and *Rosa banksiae* 'Lutea', scramble across the house walls. Beneath them there are shrub roses including 'Fantin Latour' and 'Charles de Mills' while 'Albertine' winds its way along the railings. Alongside this Alasdair is training an espalier pear – *Pyrus* 'Doyenné du Comice' – as a companion to a mature pear that covers the entire wall of an adjacent stone barn.

Voluminous pots are planted with perennials (which require far less maintenance than smaller, annual planters), including *Crambe maritima*, *Artemisia*, verbascums, gaura, *Lychnis coronaria*, *Matthiola incana* and devil's-bit scabious.

A series of clipped beech topiary domes stretches acoss the front of the house, delineating the developing wildflower meadows, which are currently Alasdair's greatest obsession. They've been adding yellow rattle here in great swathes and seeing what emerges each season as the taller grasses are gradually suppressed. In autumn their mini-flock of mixed breed sheep is brought in to graze and trample in the precious seeds. Already there's clover, *Sanguisorba* and *Scabiosa* appearing. In the meantime, the meadows have brought abundant insect life into the farm.

In late summer, the golden grasses segue gently into the surrounding rural landscape, which has been the inspiration for everything here; Alasdair likes to recite the poet Alexander Pope's advice to 'Consult the genius of the place in all', which has been a guiding principle for his approach to design, catching the distant views and bringing them into his garden. 'It was really a dream that we found this house,' he says as he surveys the meadows. 'And a dream that we bought it.'

TANIA COMPTON

WILTSHIRE

Tania Compton is experiencing the familiar feeling of those blessed with a sizeable plot, multiple careers and limited help: garden overwhelm. Alongside her current projects, conjuring grand schemes both at home and abroad, she is contributing gardens editor for *The World of Interiors*, and a long-standing trustee of London's Garden Museum. Right now she's also in the vice-like grip of her latest obsession: making natural plant dyes that colour the kaleidoscopic collection of ravishing silk panels that hang in her meadow studio.

When we meet late one summer afternoon at Spilsbury Farm in Wiltshire, she's spent the day doing back-to-back tours for a local charity around the eight-acre garden that she has created over the past 25 years. 'It often feels like I've got a thousand needy children all screaming at me', she says of the many hundred trees, shrubs and roses she's planted over that time.

When Tania arrived here with her husband, the botanist James Compton, in September 1998, the house was surrounded by tarmac and sheep meadows. Her two small children were starting school and nursery the next day. 'I got back after dropping them both off. And there was this incredible open sky, and no houses in sight. It was paradise.' For the first two years she grew vegetables, before telling the farmer that the sheep would have to go as she was planning to make a garden. 'He said, "On that soil, you'll never make a garden."

She created a central east-west axis between a *Salix alba* on a neighbouring field and a characterful old oak on the opposite side of her plot. On the line between them she planted a collection of contrasting hornbeam shapes, where two rows of *Carpinus betulus* cubes meet an avenue of *b.* 'Frans Fontaine' with an arc of *b.* 'Globus' beyond.

'I always wanted to keep this sense of being in a landscape but not contained in parcels,' Tania says of her naturalistic scheme. 'I've used trees as a note of formality in the meadow, and they're way markers so that you know where you're going.' In the adjoining meadow, a similar approach sees a circle of *Salix alba* var. *vitellina* 'Nova', which blazes like a ring of fire in winter, joined by *Crocosmia* 'Lucifer' in summer. Beyond it, two long swirls of box hedging lead to a larger grid of *Salix alba* var. *sericea*, which is pollarded every five years. Throughout the meadows there are mown paths and clearings but, she adds, 'We really do garden it with a light touch.'

Part of that low-maintenance approach are the loosely arranged perennials that are dotted through the long grasses, which she calls her 'meadow borders'. *Astrantia* 'Roma', cranesbill geraniums, *Aruncus* 'Horatio' and *Thalictrum* all tough it out here among long grasses. Pink and white forms of *Filipendula* sit alongside the lilac spires of *Veronicastrum* and later they are followed by Michaelmas daisies. *Euphorbia palustris*, which appears to love the damp conditions, is dotted in clumps through the grass, bringing lime zing before turning shrimp pink later in the season. Along with everything else here, it's all cut back by a topper in early autumn.

Tania grew up in London, although her earliest garden memories are of an old vicarage rented by her parents in Rutland that was next door to Burley on the Hill, a Palladian mansion with a Humphry Repton landscape and 'an amazing kitchen

'WE REALLY DO GARDEN IT WITH A LIGHT TOUCH.'

garden with crinkle crankle walls, peach houses and sunken tomato houses'. But nothing in her childhood suggested she might work with plants. After school, she moved to Paris to work as an assistant at *Women's Wear Daily* where, she says, she had an 'amazing interiors and gardens kind of education', filing the editor's stories on Hubert de Givenchy's garden or Nicole de Vésian's La Louve.

It wasn't until she spent time in Ibiza that Tania was 'hijacked by nature'. When she returned to the UK, a friend of her mother's suggested she contact an old friend, Penelope Hobhouse. She spent a summer working at Tintinhull, the National Trust property where Penelope lived with her husband John Malins from 1980 until 1993: 'Penny would say "This is what you should read." Or "Go and visit this garden, or that garden." She was phenomenal and so generous.'

This proved to be her garden awakening. Penelope introduced her to the plantswoman Patricia Marrow and a job at East Lambrook Manor followed, even if her friends were astonished that she'd traded a glamorous party lifestyle for 6 a.m. starts and £25 a week working as a gardener. She met Nori and Sandra Pope, who were creating magic at Hadspen House in Somerset: 'I saw this beautiful couple making what was the most incredible garden I think I've ever been to, or ever will,' Tania remembers. 'By this stage I was fanatical. It was all I wanted to do.'

A course at The English Gardening School followed, where she met James, who was head gardener of the Chelsea Physic Garden where the school is based. They were married in 1989 and moved out of London to a house in Wylye valley, Wiltshire. Her garden there had 'every trick in the book. I was basically trying everything, but I look back on it and I think, "My God, the energy and the creativity."'

Tania was also designing clients' gardens, but by the time she had her first child in 1992 it became impossible to continue. She'd already been writing for *House & Garden* and the new editor, Sue Crewe, offered her a role as gardens editor. By the time she arrived at Spilsbury Farm, she'd spent the best part of the 1990s involved in the most exciting horticultural happenings, meeting new and established designers and immersing herself in research. Now her accumulated knowledge and experience were poured into her vast new garden. Her stint at East Lambrook Manor gardens inspired a Mediterranean terrace of silver-leaved plants in the front of her house, where santolina, gaura, perovskia, eryngiums, stachys and lavender thrive despite the leaden clay soil and north-facing position. Close to this, along a wall *Dianthus* 'Memories' is arranged in terracotta pots 'at nose level' so their delicious fresh-laundry scent can be easily appreciated.

An orchard was planted featuring many varities of apple, including Jamie's favourite 'Spartan' and 'Keswick Codlin', which she describes as the best cooker on the planet. Underneath the apple trees a sea of spring bulbs begins with snowdrops before fritillaries and a succession of camassias flower under the blossom in the long grass.

Nothing here looks too cultivated. In the meadow, Tania shares a key tip for establishing structure by planting young box plants at the same time as rugosa roses, creating sculptural hedges topped with single roses.

Wild or rambling roses including 'Rambling Rector', 'Ethel' or 'Venusta Pendula' are planted in the meadows or close to trees where they can scramble up into the highest branches. Through growing hundreds of varieties Tania has learnt which tend to be less appealing to the deer here; 'Dupontii', a shrub rose with white single flowers, the delicious pink 'Ispahan', which is dotted through the garden, the glorious scarlet Gallica rose, 'Scharlachglut' and 'Rose de Rescht' ('a modern rose that looks like an old rose') have all proven to be less of a tempting snack for passing wildlife.

There's still the 'odd diva', including *R.* 'Madame Legras de Saint Germain' – a double creamy white shrub rose with delicious mossy buds. Or in more formal beds close to the house, there is the luscious 'Sharifa Asma' – a pinky-peach David Austin shrub rose with a fruity tea rose scent.

Beyond the meadows there's the deep shade of the nut walk, submerged in water for much of the winter, and underplanted with lush ferns and swathes of snowdrops. Close by are two large ponds, edged with purple loosestrife, bullrushes and flag iris. On misty late summer mornings, kingfishers swoop down into the water here. For Tania, who often sleeps in an old gypsy wagon in the field in the summer months, it's the ultimate place to be.

SELECTED PLANT LISTS

Tom Stuart-Smith
Alcea rugosa
Aralia cordata
Campanula lactiflora 'Prichard's Variety'
Digitalis ferruginea
Doellingeria umbellata
Euphorbia margalidiana, E. mellifera
Eryngium x zabelii
Genista aetnensis
Knautia arvensis
Lilium henryi
Macleaya cordata
Valeriana officinalis
Veronicastrum virginicum 'Erica'

Miranda Brooks
Achillea 'Credo'
Alchemilla mollis
Bistorta amplexicaulis 'Alba'
Clematis tangutica 'Bill MacKenzie'
Dahlia 'Café au Lait', *D.* 'Preference', *D.* 'Apache'
Digitalis lutea
Patrinia scabiosifolia
Rosa 'Tottering-by-Gently', *R.* 'Yellow Mutabilis'
Scabiosa ochroleuca
Selinum wallichianum
Stipa calamagrostis

Dan Pearson
Athamantha turbith
Bupleurum falcatum
Calamagrostis acutiflora 'Karl Foerster'
Convolvulus cneorum
Dianthus carthusianorum
Digitalis lutea
Ferula communis
Gunnera manicata
Nepeta 'Blue Dragon'
Oenothera stricta 'Sulphurea'
Phlomis italica
Rosa soulieana
Salix purpurea 'Nancy Saunders'
Salvia sclarea 'Vatican White'
Salvia x jamensis 'Heatwave Glimmer'
Stipa tenuissima
Tetrapanax papyrifer 'Rex'
Thalictrum flavum subsp. glaucum
Verbascum olympicum 'Arctic Summer'

Harry and David Rich
Artemesia lactiflora
Bistorta amplexicaulis 'Alba'
Deschampsia cespitosa
Digitalis ferruginea
Eupatorium maculatum 'Atropurpureum'
Hamamelis x intermedia 'Jelena'
Kalimeris incisa 'Alba'
Malus 'Evereste'
Molinia 'Transparent'
Nepeta govaniana, N. nuda 'Romany Dusk'
Sanguisorba 'Korean Snow'
Scabiosa ochroleuca
Selinum wallichianum
Thalictrum 'Black Stockings', *T.* 'Elin' *and T.* 'Splendide White'
Verbascum chaixii 'Album'
Veronicastrum virginicum 'Album'

Sarah Price
Calamintha nepeta 'Blue Cloud'
Cistus x *argenteus* 'Silver Pink'
Euphorbia margalidiana, E. rigida, E. seguieriana subsp. *niciciana*
Ligusticum lucidum
Lotus hirsutus
Mimulus luteus
Oenothera stricta 'Sulphurea'
Origanum laevigatum 'Herrenhausen'
Pastinaca sativa
Pennisetum macrourum
Rosa x odorata 'Bengal Crimson' and *R.* x *odorata* 'Mutabilis'
Salvia candelabrum
Scabiosa ochroleuca 'Moon Dance'
Crambe maritima
Sesleria nitida
Stipa splendens

Nigel Dunnett
Achillea 'Terracotta'
Astilbe chinensis var.taquetii 'Purpurlanze'
Athyrium filix-femina
Betula papyrifera
Campanula lactiflora
Carex elata 'Aurea'
Carex x oshimensis 'Evergold'
Crocosmia x crocosmiiflora 'Solfatare'
Deschampsia cespitosa
Geranium sylvaticum
Geum 'Lemon Drops'
Hakonechloa
Helictotrichon sempervirens
Iris sibirica
Leucanthemum x superbum 'Becky'
Melica uniflora f.albida
Miscanthus x giganteus
Sorbus aucuparia
Thalictrum 'Elin'

Sheila Jack
Allium angulosum 'Summer Beauty'
Agastache 'Blue Fortune'
Calamagrostis brachytricha
Dianthus carthusianorum
Echinacea pallida 'Hula Dancer'
Eryngium bourgatii, E. yuccifolium
Helenium 'Moerheim Beauty'
Hylotelephium 'Matrona'
Liatris pycnostachya
Nepeta nuda 'Romany Dusk'
Panicum virgatum 'Shenandoah'
Pennisetum alopecuroides 'Red Head'
Rosa pimpinellifolia
Sesleria autumnalis
Sisyrinchium striatum
Sporobolus heterolepis
Stachys byzantina 'Silver Carpet'
Succisella inflexa 'Frosted Pearls'
Succisa pratensis
Veronicastrum virginicum 'Album'

Chris Moss
Agastache phoeniculum 'Alabaster'
Allium tuberosum
Althaea cannabina
Ammi majus
Anemone japonica 'Prinz Heinrich'
Aster x frikartii 'Mönch'
Bistorta amplexicaulis 'Rosea'
Disporum longistylum 'Night Heron'
Kirengeshoma palmata
Molinia 'Heidebraut'
Molinia caerulea 'Karl Foerster'
Rhynchospora colorata
Rodgersia podophylla
Rosa 'Mrs Oakley Fisher'
Salvia x jamensis 'Nachtvlinder'
Sanguisorba 'All Time High'
Scabiosa ochroleuca
Succisella inflexa 'Frosted Pearls'
Symphyotrichum 'Little Carlow'

Arne Maynard
Taxus baccata
Fagus sylvatica f. *purpurea*
Malus 'Evereste'
R. 'Jude the Obscure', *R.* 'Perle d'Or', *R.* 'Sir Paul Smith'
Iris 'Benton Susan›
Iris hollandica 'Autumn Princess'
Trollius 'Lemon Queen'
Bistorta officianlis
Digitalis parviflora
Leucanthemum vulgare
Paeonia mlokosewitschii
Anthriscus sylvestris 'Ravenswing'
Verbascum phoeniceum 'Violetta'
Achillea ageratum
Paeonia 'Prairie Moon'
Geranium pratense 'Summer Skies'
Linaria 'Canon Went'

Arabella Lennox-Boyd
Althaea cannabina
Artemisia lactiflora 'Guizhou'
Carex elata 'Aurea'
Cornus kousa 'Miss Satomi', *C.* 'John Slocock', *C.* 'Norman Hadden'
Cotinus coggygria 'Atropurpureus'
Davidia involucrata
Erigeron annuus
Geranium x oxonianum 'Rebecca Moss', *G. psilostemon*
Molinia 'Transparent'
Paeonia mlokosewitschii
Phlox paniculata 'Fujiyama', *P.* 'Blue Boy'
Prunus lusitanica
Pyrus amygdaliformis, P. salicifolia
Rosa 'Buff Beauty', *Rosa* 'Roseraie de l'Haye', *R.* 'Sanders' White', *R.* 'Tuscany Superb'
Salix lanata
Thalictrum 'Elin'
Veronica 'Shirley Blue'

Butter Wakefield
Allium 'Purple Rain'
Aquilegia caerulea 'Rose Queen'
Chaenomeles speciosa 'Nivalis'
Echium vulgare
Geranium 'Ann Folkard', *G. pyrenaicum* 'Bill Wallis'
Geum 'Totally Tangerine'
Magnolia grandiflora
Molinia 'Transparent', *M.* 'Heidebraut'
Myrtus communis
Nepeta govaniana
Osmanthus x burkwoodii
Silene dioica
Taxus baccata
Trachelospermum jasminoides
Verbena bonariensis

Mary Keen
Anemone blanda, A. pavonina
Coronilla glauca 'Citrina'
Daphne bholua 'Jacqueline Postill'
Euphorbia characias subsp. wulfenii
Gladiolus byzantinus
Lunaria annua 'Corfu Blue'
Magnolia x soulangeana, M. liliiflora
Narcissus 'Segovia'
Primula elatior, P. veris
Rosa 'Paul's Himalayan Musk', R. x odorata 'Mutabilis', *R.* 'Bengal Crimson'
Tulipa acuminata

Catherine FitzGerald
Alchemilla erythropoda, A. mollis
Centranthus ruber var. coccineus
Cynara cardunculus
Dryopteris filix mas
Erysimum 'Bowles Mauve'
Euphorbia wallichii
Knautia macedonica
Ligusticum lucidum
Lonicera etrusca 'Michael Rosse'
Macleaya cordata
Onopordum acanthium
Paeonia lactiflora 'Duchesse de Nemours'
Papaver rupifragum 'Orange Ruffles'
Phlomis fruticosa
Rosa 'Cécile Brünner', *R.* 'Cornelia', *R.* 'Félicité Perpétue', *R.* 'Francis E. Lester', *R.* 'Paul's Himalayan Musk', *R. x odorata* 'Mutabilis'
Salvia officinalis 'Berggarten'

Isabel and Julian Bannerman
Cardiocrinum giganteum
Crambe cordifolia
Daphne odora
Erigeron karvinskianus
Euphorbia characias subsp. wulfenii
Lavandula angustifolia
Leucanthemum x superbum
Lilium martagon 'Peppard Gold'
Lupinus 'The Page'
Phlox paniculata 'David'
Rosa 'Madame Alfred Carrière', *R.* 'Perennial Blue', *R.* 'The Garland', *R.* 'Tuscany Superb'
Salvia rosmarinus
Taxus baccata
Thalictrum 'Splendide White'

Libby Russell
Aster x frikartii 'Mönch'
Betonica officinalis 'Rosea Superba'
Cephalaria gigantea
Dianthus carthusianorum
Eryngium 'Cobalt Star'
Knautia macedonica 'Melton Pastels'
Nepeta nuda 'Romany Dusk', *N.* 'Six Hills Giant'
Patrinia scabiosifolia
Phlomisoides tuberosa 'Amazone'
Rosa 'Lyda Rose', *R.* 'Kew Gardens', *R. pimpinellifolia* 'Mary Rose', *R.* 'Sally Holmes', *R.* 'Trier'
R. 'Vanity'
Rudbeckia subtomentosa 'Henry Eilers'
Salvia pratensis 'Indigo'
Sanguisorba 'Pink Tanna'
Selinum wallichianum
Sesleria 'Greenlee'
Succisa pratensis 'Derby Purple'
Veronicastrum virginicum 'Erica'

Emily Erlam
Ballota pseudodictamnus
Buddleja davidii 'Black Knight'
Cercis canadensis 'Forest Pansy'
Choisya x dewitteana 'Aztec Pearl'
Cornus kousa var. chinensis
Echium pininana
Tetrapanax papyrifer 'Rex'
Edgeworthia chrysantha
Fatsia japonica
Fuchsia magellanica var. molinae
Ilex crenata
Luma apiculata
Melianthus major
Melica altissima 'Alba'
Pittosporum tenuifolium 'Golf Ball'
Rosa x odorata 'Mutabilis', *R.* 'Cécile Brünner', *R.* 'Pierre de Ronsard'
Stachyurus praecox
Trachelospermum jasminoides

Alasdair Cameron
Calamintha nepeta
Deschampsia cespitosa
Eryngium yuccifolium
Eupatorium atropuroureum Purpurea
Eurybia schreberi
Foeniculum vulgare
Miscanthus x giganteus
Molinia caerulea 'Heidebraut'
Eryngium pandanifolium.
Phlox paniculata
Salvia involucrata 'Hadspen'
Succisa pratensis
Verbascum chaixii 'Album', *V. hastata, V. olympicum*
Vernonia arkansana

Tania Compton
Carpinus betulus, b. 'Frans Fontaine', *b.* 'Globus'
Salix alba var. vitellina 'Nova',
Crocosmia 'Lucifer'
Salix alba var. sericea,
Astrantia 'Roma'
cranesbill geraniums
Aruncus 'Horatio'
Thalictrum
Filipendula
Veronicastrum
Euphorbia palustris
Rosa 'Dupontii', *R.* 'Ethel', *R.* 'Ispahan', *R.* 'Madame Legras de Saint Germain', *R.* 'Rambling Rector', *R.* 'Rose de Rescht', *R.* 'Scharlachglut', *R.* 'Sharifa Asma', *R.* 'Venusta Pendula'

ACKNOWLEDGEMENTS

The gasp test may not be a very scientific way to assess a garden's merits, but a sharp intake of breath when faced, for the first time, with an unexplored garden is a pretty good assessment of its power to transport us. There have been many gasps in the making of this book.

My heartfelt thanks to all the designers who generously allowed us into their private gardens, some of which have not been photographed before, and for giving up their precious time for portraits and interviews. It's a joy to be a garden writer, but even more so when quizzing some of the world's greatest designers on their process and planting philosophy.

For me the best gardens are all about atmosphere and how they make you feel, and it's often impossible to capture that multi-sensory experience in still images. Somehow Éva Németh captures it every time. Seeing a garden through her eyes, and collaborating with her on this book, has been an absolute pleasure from start to finish. Thank you to Eve Marleau at Quadrille for commissioning this beautiful book, and for putting up with my relentless pursuit of a cloth cover. Thanks also to Daniel New for his wonderful design and to Gillian Haslam for her brilliant light touch copy edit. Lastly thank you to Derren Gilhooley, my forever gardening guru and long-suffering sounding board, he was doing the same thing twenty years ago when I wrote my first book.

I hope everyone who reads this book enjoys it, as much as we have enjoyed making it.

Clare Coulson is a journalist specialising in landscape design, gardens and horticulture, for titles including the *Financial Times, Daily Telegraph, House & Garden, Condé Nast Traveller, The English Garden* and *Gardenista*. She is co-editor and contributing writer of *Blooms* and *The Garden Chef*. She is also a lecturer in journalism at Central Saint Martins in London. In a former life she was Fashion Editor at the *Daily Telegraph* and Fashion Features Director at *Harper's Bazaar* before moving to the country, becoming obsessed with plants and developing her own one acre garden on the Suffolk coast.

Quadrille, Penguin Random House UK,
One Embassy Gardens, 8 Viaduct Gardens, London SW11 7BW

Quadrille Publishing Limited is part of the Penguin Random House group of companies whose addresses can be found at global.penguinrandomhouse.com

Published by Quadrille in 2025

www.penguin.co.uk

A CIP catalogue record for this book is available from the British Library

ISBN 978-1-78488794-0
10 9 8 7 6 5 4 3 2 1

Publishing Director: Kate Pollard
Commissioning Editor: Eve Marleau
Photographer: Éva Németh
Designer: Daniel New
Copy Editor: Gillian Haslam
Proofreader: Lucy Kingett
Production Director: Stephen Lang
Production Controller: Martina Georgieva

Colour reproduction by p2d

Printed in China by C&C Offset Printing Co., Ltd.

The authorised representative in the EEA is Penguin Random House Ireland, Morrison Chambers, 32 Nassau Street, Dublin D02 YH68.

Penguin Random House is committed to a sustainable future for our business, our readers and our planet. This book is made from Forest Stewardship Council® certified paper.